Ripe

A FRESH, COLORFUL APPROACH TO FRUITS AND VEGETABLES

CHERYL STERNMAN RULE

PHOTOGRAPHY BY
PAULETTE PHLIPOT

RUNNING PRESS
PHILADELPHIA · LONDON

Central Rappaho... Regional Library
...
Street
...VA 22401

641
34
Rue
C.7

Text © 2011 by Cheryl Sternman Rule
Photography © 2011 by Paulette Phlipot

All rights reserved under the Pan-American and International Copyright Conventions.
Printed in China

*This book may not be reproduced in whole or in part, in any form or by any means, electronic or
mechanical, including photocopying, recording, or by any information storage and retrieval system now known
or hereafter invented, without written permission from the publisher.*

Books published by Running Press are available at special discounts for bulk purchases in the United States
by corporations, institutions, and other organizations. For more information, please contact the Special Markets
Department at the Perseus Books Group, 2300 Chestnut Street, Suite 200, Philadelphia, PA 19103, or
call (800) 810-4145, ext. 5000, or e-mail special.markets@perseusbooks.com.

ISBN 978-0-7624-4024-5
Library of Congress Control Number: 2011939380

E-book ISBN 978-0-7624-4497-7

9   8   7   6   5   4   3   2
Digit on the right indicates the number of this printing

Book design by Amanda Richmond
Edited by Geoffrey Stone

Running Press Book Publishers
2300 Chestnut Street
Philadelphia, PA 19103-4371

Visit us on the web!
www.runningpresscooks.com

To Colin

and to Rudy

Contents

Acknowledgments

I offer my gratitude to all the friends and family who stood behind me as I completed the photography for this book. Pouring my passion for fruits and vegetables into a project like this is something I have thought about for many years.

Meeting Cheryl Sternman Rule reignited this passion. After setting eyes on her writing, I knew she was capable of bringing a fresh enthusiasm to produce, which is so everyday to most, but which I have always adored. I could not have imagined working with a more talented or creative food writer for this book.

I thank my parents for sharing their love for gardening and good food with me. I also thank my husband Rudy for his enthusiasm and for always keeping an eye out for the best looking produce at the market (and for always asking, "Can I eat this or do you want to photograph it first?") Finally, to my baby Cassidy: I so look forward to being in the kitchen with you, cooking and eating the recipes in this book together.

—Paulette Phlipot

A smorgasbord of magnificent people helped me turn a rather vague artistic vision into the book you now hold in your hands. Let me introduce you to them.

First is Paulette Phlipot. Paulette has been my partner-in-crime from the get-go, and without her creativity, talent, patience, and easygoing disposition, this book simply wouldn't exist. Her photography inspired me from this project's pre-beginning to its final instant and at each incremental point in between. I couldn't imagine a better copilot.

Paulette and I would jointly like to thank our candid, kind, and ever-responsive superagent Jenni Ferrari-Adler of Brick House Literary Agents. Jenni expertly shepherded us through the minutiae of book dealdom and beyond, and we continue to benefit greatly from her counsel and encouragement. Joint thanks, too, to our editor, Geoffrey Stone, and the terrific designer Amanda Richmond at Running Press. Geoff allowed us to fill this book with a huge number of color photographs, something for which we are especially grateful. A tip of the hat as well to indexer Suzanne Fass, a consummate professional in all realms.

We'd also like to thank the many farmers not only in and around Sun Valley and San Jose, where we make our respective homes, but to farmers everywhere. Without their efforts, we would not have been inspired to walk this particular path, and the book in front of you might be about packing material instead of produce.

To my dream team of recipe testers: Cheryl Arkison, Katrina Brinkman, Erika Bruner, Jacqui Gal Cohen, Meloni Courtway, Stacy Dobner, Kate Fichter, Cynthia Graber, Elisa Koff-Ginsborg, Don Lesser, Kathleen Lingo, Katharine Norwood, April Paffrath, Liz Phillips, Diana Pisciotta, Susan Russo, Julia Schiff, Elaine Schultz, Melissa Shafer, Jennifer Simons, Jackie Vail, Heather Walker, and Dana Wootton — I offer you all a curtsy of gratitude so deep I fall over. Thanks too to friends Alison Brunner, Andrea Mello, and Liz Linehan, and to farmers' market vendors Grace Vanoyan Yepremian and Donna Borchard.

Special thanks to Tara Mataraza Desmond, Lisa Hoffman, and my sister Julie Sternman, who not only tested recipes but provided invaluable feedback and support during some hairy times toward the end; I am forever in your debt. To my dear friends Jill O'Connor and Denise Marchessault: thank you for contributing recipes for Roasted Pumpkin Gingerbread and Mango with Lime Crème Anglaise, respectively, and for your tremendous friendship.

To my brothers, Mark and Matt, my father, Joel, and my stepmother, Barbara: thank you for your keen editorial eyes and words of long-standing praise and encouragement. And to my in-laws Clifton, Ian, and Beth: thank you for all the support.

Finally, to my husband, Colin, and my sons, Andrew and Alex: feeding you feeds me. I could not ask for better stomachs to fill, or for better souls with whom to share each day of my life.
—Cheryl Sternman Rule

Introduction

The first time I saw an iPhone was in the lobby of a New Orleans hotel when a food photographer I'd just met named Paulette Phlipot asked if I wanted to see her portfolio. I nodded, and in an instant, my professional world changed.

The screen showcased ripe cherries, purple eggplant, and tall blades of wheat. Weathered farmers, hearty entrées, and tables set for twelve. I wanted to blow up Paulette's photos and tack them to the ceiling. I wanted to meet that farmer, to sit at that table. But most of all, I wanted to pluck those cherries from her screen and thrust them in my mouth, all at once, stems, pits, and all. I wanted to lick her touchpad.

Eventually I handed the phone back, but those photographs had left their mark. Paulette has the ability to make colors pop, to make textures dimensional, to tell a fully realized story through her skillful command of the lens. And her facility at showcasing the natural purity of food, particularly of fruits and vegetables, moved me deeply.

The genesis of this book happened there in that hotel lobby, though neither of us knew it at the time.

While I'm a classic omnivore and Paulette eats fish, we both prefer the freshness, flavor, and simplicity of produce. On any day of the week, at any time of the day, we'd just rather make out with a juicy watermelon than a floppy piece of chicken.

If you like meat, go ahead and eat it. I'm not here to judge, much as I hope you won't judge me. But do embrace the vegetable; behold the fruit. Not because they're good for you, though they are. Not because their footprint is lighter on the earth, though it is. Not because a pound of snap peas costs less than a pound of tenderloin, though it does. Gorge on green beans and favas, pomegranates and peaches, Swiss chard and honeydew because they're beautiful, flavorful, versatile, and undeniably delicious. Canoodle them because you crave what they offer— freshness, color, snap, and taste. Kiss them, love them, hug them, squeeze them, and enjoy them morning, noon, and night.

Don't eat your fruits and veggies because your mama told you to. Eat them because you want them in every sense of the word. Because seeing them in the market, at the produce stand, on an iPhone, or in the pages of a cookbook accelerates your pulse and makes you very, very hungry.

What This Book Isn't, and What It Is

Many, if not most, produce-centered cookbooks are organized by season, and with good reason: seasonal eating makes sense from an environmental, fiscal, and culinary point of view. I eat seasonally, and I encourage you to as well. But this is not a seasonal eating book.

Many books also explain why you should eat more fruits and vegetables. They recount studies about how diets lower in animal products protect your heart, slash obesity, tread lighter on the earth, and are more ethically sound. And I don't disagree. Not a bit. In fact, I've spent years as a food writer penning these stories myself and believe deeply in these messages. But this book is different. It's not a health-focused prescription. It's not an environmental screed.

So relax. Soften your shoulders. What you'll find in these pages is sensory, pretty, practical, and fun. Why? Because those other, more serious books have already been written, and written quite well. Consumers and diners already know that they should be eating more fruits, vegetables, and whole grains; that they should be consuming fewer overall calories; that they should be sourcing their food more consciously and responsibly. They don't need to be told again and again and again.

So I'm glossing over the shoulds. I'm presuming you know them, and I respect your ability to make your own choices about what foods you're willing to include in your diet and why. Instead, I want to excite you and show you a good time. By presenting stories, photographs, recipes, and practical, flavorful ingredient combinations, I'm hoping you'll pick up that pomegranate because you genuinely want to eat it, not because it's low in calories or rich in vitamin C or because studies show it blah blah blahs. I want you to crave that pomegranate, or that peach, or that head of ivory cauliflower. I want you to reach for the bok choy because you finally know how to prep it, and aren't afraid it's going to shrivel and die before you figure out how to cook it. I want to show you how to make an hors d'oeuvre with nothing more than a few radishes and some crusty bread, or a simple tart with a tangled mess of onions, some sun-dried tomatoes, and a shower of finely shredded cheese.

I want you to love produce because—well, simply because you love it.

Not because you should.

What are Simple Uses For ?

In addition to photos and complete recipes, you will also see three Simple Uses For each featured produce item. These quick-hit ingredient combos are just that: ideas to jump-start your own creative process when considering each fruit and vegetable. They are not full-fledged recipes, but rather a fast, easy way to begin exploring compatible flavors and become inspired. Feel free to search your favorite culinary websites (there are so many!) for how to execute the suggested dishes to your liking. I'll be right there, in spirit, cheering you on from the sidelines.

A note about lemons, salt, eggs, oil, puppies, chocolate, and coconut

As the proud owner of a Meyer lemon tree, I use these mild, low-acid citrus fruits in my recipes when they're in season. Where I call for lemons, therefore, please always adjust the amount to suit your taste, especially if you're using the more widely available Eureka variety.

By the same token, salt is always kosher (unless coarse salt is specified), eggs are large, and olive oil is extra virgin. Also, puppies are cute, chocolate is delicious, and I really, really, really like coconut.

RED

Beets

Imagine pulling a beet from the earth. It looks like a dirty, bulbous ball with stringy entrails. If you didn't know better, you might pass it up in favor of something cleaner looking—a shiny tomato, say, or a gobstopper. But reconsider. Once scrubbed and prepped for the plate, beets undergo a miraculous aesthetic and culinary transformation. When blasted with an oven's dry heat, they sweeten considerably, so roasting is a popular method for coaxing forth their natural sugars. And while some people steam or boil them, I think this makes them taste too much like feet, so my strong personal preference is either to roast them or eat them raw. In fresh, crisp slaws or when you shave them ultra thin, you get a bonus crunch, all that glorious color, and a sweetness that doesn't smack of trodden mud. *Tip:* If you buy impeccably fresh beets, go ahead and toss the leaves in salads, or sauté or braise them as you would other greens.

SIMPLE USES FOR BEETS:

composed salad = roasted beets + burrata cheese + beluga lentils + walnut oil
slaw = shredded raw beets + carrots + red cabbage + red apple + red onion + cider vinaigrette
pickled beets = beets + sherry vinegar + allspice + bay leaf + peppercorns + sugar + water

Shaved Chioggia Beet Salad with Mixed Citrus Vinaigrette

This salad couldn't be lovelier, unless it were wearing a sparkly tiara. Slice the beets—
Chioggas are sometimes called candy striped or candy cane beets—as thinly as possible.

SERVES 4 TO 6

Finely shredded zest and juice of ½ lemon

Finely shredded zest and juice of ½ lime

Finely shredded zest and juice of ½ orange

2 tablespoons extra-virgin olive oil

½ teaspoon sugar

Kosher salt and freshly ground pepper

6 small Chioggia beets, trimmed and peeled (reserve greens for another use)

¼ cup (40g) golden raisins, slivered

1 large head frisée, or other tender salad greens, sliced crosswise

¼ cup (1oz) crumbled goat cheese

Coarse salt, for sprinkling

Combine the citrus zest from all three fruit halves in a small bowl. Set aside.

Combine the lemon, lime, and orange juices in the bottom of a large salad bowl. (You should have about ¼ cup, or 60ml juice.) Slowly whisk in the olive oil, the sugar, ¼ teaspoon kosher salt, and a generous grinding of pepper. Taste, and adjust the seasonings (especially the sugar) if necessary. Transfer half of the dressing to a small dish.

Carefully shave the beets into thin slices using a mandoline on its thinnest setting, or a vegetable peeler. You want to expose the beets' concentric circles, so shave horizontally across the bottom of the beets. Transfer to the salad bowl.

Add the raisins and frisée. Toss to coat. Sprinkle with the goat cheese and a few pinches of the mixed citrus zest. Adjust seasonings to taste, adding a bit of the reserved vinaigrette, if desired. (Any leftover vinaigrette and zest may be stored, separately, in the refrigerator for several days.) Sprinkle with the coarse salt. Serve immediately.

Blood Oranges

Pity the blood orange's violent name; it's actually quite a peaceful fruit.

Most often associated with Sicily, where they abound in simple desserts and salads, blood oranges boast deeply pigmented flesh thanks to anthocyanins, those same compounds found in blackberries and purple cabbage. Eat them for their bright and balanced citrus flavor, a flavor sometimes called berrylike. I personally think they taste like oranges, only a bit more complex.

Play up their bold, unique color by keeping preparations clean. Tuscan kale with blood orange, a tall glass of fresh juice, a blood orange tossed in a lunchbox. Just imagine the fun a fourth-grade boy could have in the cafeteria when he peels one for his buddies. "It's so blooooooooooooooooooooooody."

Tip: Look for heavy blood oranges with scarlet color visible in patches on the peel.

SIMPLE USES FOR BLOOD ORANGES:

classic Sicilian preparation *=* blood oranges + red onions + olive oil

sorbet *=* blood orange juice + sugar + vanilla bean

salad *=* blood oranges + spinach + roasted beets + olives + blood orange vinaigrette

Boozy Blood Oranges

This dessert makes a light, sophisticated,
and stunning finale to a heavy winter meal.
Serve it in shallow bowls so you can lap up any
residual liqueur like a thirsty dog.

SERVES 4

4 blood oranges

2 tablespoons amaretto liqueur

¹⁄₄ cup (55g) Marcona almonds, finely chopped

Using a sharp knife, carefully remove the peel and white pith from the blood oranges. Cut the oranges into thick circles and arrange decoratively on a platter. Drizzle with the liqueur and set aside for 5 minutes. Sprinkle with the almonds and serve immediately.

Cherries

Warning: if you don't wear an apron when pitting cherries, you'll look like you've killed someone. Also, it's tempting to pop them in your mouth as you work. One for you, one for the bowl. Three for you, one for the bowl. Eight for you, one for the bowl. After thirty minutes, your bowl will hold about two and a half cherries.

Cherry season is relatively short, so each summer, buy pounds and pounds of cherries to toss both in sweet dishes, where they're expected, and savory ones, where they're not. Garnet, Brooks, Rainier, Bing—chuck them all in your bag, filling it with sweet, happy weight.

When their final week arrives, set aside several hours to pit the last, red batch, preparing them for a cryonic nap in the freezer. It's tiring work, this cherry-slaughter, but worth the investment. Months later, when you crave a warm cherry crisp, you'll feel quite smug. A soothsayer, you'll spoon up summer in a bowl, as the wind howls and whips just outside your door.
Tip: Buy fresh cherries only at their seasonal peak. They should be firm, unblemished, and shiny, without pocks or soft spots. Seek out those with stems still attached.

SIMPLE USES FOR CHERRIES:

frozen yogurt = minced cherries + whole milk yogurt + sugar + lemon juice
green salad = cherries + baby spinach + spiced nuts + goat cheese + balsamic vinaigrette
grain salad = mixed cherries + wild or red rice + almond oil + raspberry vinegar + mint

Smashed Cherries, Amaretti and Ricotta

This no-cook summer dessert pushes cherries center stage, where they belong.
Serve it up in clear glasses and give yourself the biggest one.

SERVES 4

4 cups (1 to 1¼ pounds, 450g to 480g) fresh red cherries, stemmed

¾ cup (170g) whole milk ricotta

2 teaspoons sugar

4 teaspoons milk

½ teaspoon almond extract

4 amaretti cookies

1 teaspoon cacao nibs, or mini chocolate chips

Thwack the cherries with the flat side of a heavy knife so they flatten. Discard the pits. Divide the cherries among 4 pretty, clear glasses.

In a small bowl, stir together the ricotta, sugar, milk, and almond extract. Spoon pillows of ricotta over the cherries in equal proportions. Crumble one amaretti cookie over each serving and sprinkle with the cacao nibs. Serve immediately.

Tip: You'll find amaretti cookies (Italian macaroons) in larger supermarkets or Italian grocery stores, though you may substitute toasted, chopped almonds if you like. Then you can eat this dish for breakfast.

Cranberries

An oceanfront room in South Beach or Tortola appeals to some. The blue sky, the blue sea, blue, blue, blue. Yawn. What I'd really like, what I'd far prefer, is a room in New England looking out on a cranberry bog.

Each fall, millions of pounds of cranberries are harvested from bogs in a dozen states. While wet-harvested berries end up in commercial sauces and juices, others, bound for plastic bags, are plucked by metal-toothed machines. I picture Jaws from *Moonraker* holding this job. Hailed for their health properties—cranberry juice can help fight infection—and sacred place at the Thanksgiving table, these fruits have much more to offer than antioxidants, vitamins, and a storied North American lineage. They punch up sauces, chutneys, and desserts with their no-holds-barred flavor, leaving dramatic, tart bursts in their wine-colored wake.

Tip: Cranberries freeze beautifully and can be tough to source during nonpeak times. Buy extra bags in season and tuck them near the ice cream.

SIMPLE USES FOR CRANBERRIES:

tea bread = fresh and dried cranberries + flour + baking soda + pumpkin pie spice + eggs + brown sugar + pumpkin purée + oil

cooked cranberry sauce = cranberries + honey + brown sugar + water + star anise + cinnamon + Grand Marnier

raw cranberry applesauce = cranberries + apples + orange + honey + cinnamon + cardamom

Cranberry Apple Butter

Thanks to the slow cooker, this festive, burgundy spread comes together effortlessly.
Slather it on holiday breads, muffins, or scones, or spoon some into the
Pomegranate Clove Thumbprint Cookies on page 32.

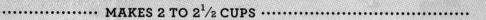 **MAKES 2 TO 2$\frac{1}{2}$ CUPS**

1 (12-ounce, 340g) bag cranberries, fresh or frozen (unthawed), rinsed briefly

2 medium red apples (Pink Lady, for example), peeled, cored and roughly chopped

$\frac{3}{4}$ teaspoon ground cinnamon

$\frac{1}{2}$ teaspoon unsweetened cocoa powder

2 tablespoons cranberry or apple juice, cider, or water

$\frac{3}{4}$ cup to 1 cup (188g to 250g) granulated sugar

2 tablespoons unsalted butter, melted

Combine the cranberries, apples, cinnamon, cocoa, juice or water, and sugar (use the larger amount if you prefer sweeter spreads, the smaller amount if you enjoy a tart bite) in a slow cooker. Cover, turn on low heat, and cook for 8 to 10 hours (see Tip).

Using a potato masher, slowly but carefully mash the fruit to a thick and even consistency, leaving a few berries whole, if desired, for a tart burst of flavor. Cool until just warm, about 1 hour. Whisk in the melted butter until incorporated.

Serve immediately, or cool to room temperature, cover and refrigerate for several hours or overnight. (May be stored, refrigerated, for up to two weeks, tightly covered.)

Tip: When using a 6-quart (or smaller) slow cooker, cook the butter for 10 hours. If using a larger one, check it after 8.

Grapefruit

When I was young, my family appetized. No silver trays, no frouffy caviar. These starters were modest, quick, straightforward affairs: canned soup and fruit cocktail in heavy rotation with melon wedges or grapefruit halves. Those tart grapefruits would cut through my tongue like nails through a two by four unless I went to town with the honey, so go to town I did. I went to town and back, and then I went to town again. I lived in town, basically.

To this day, I still believe deeply in the grapefruit-honey yin-yang. It's not a religion per se, but a firm belief that they go together. Like ramma lamma lamma ka dinga da dinga dong.

Tip: I highly recommend adding a few serrated grapefruit spoons to your silverware drawer. Not only are they ideal for serving grapefruit, but you'll use the spoons for everything from scraping out pumpkins to seeding melons.

SIMPLE USES FOR GRAPEFRUIT:

marmalade = grapefruit juice + lemon juice + orange juice + sugar + pectin

salad = baby spinach + avocado + grapefruit + jicama + champagne vinaigrette

broiled grapefruit = grapefruit halves + maple syrup (even better: maple sugar, if you've got it)

Grapefruit Honey Sorbet

This pretty pink sorbet, so elegant, so proper, gets a big smack of ginger at serving time.
The more membrane you can remove from the fruit, the smoother your results will be.

······················· **SERVES 4** ·······················

3 ruby red grapefruits
   (about 1 pound, 16oz, each)

²/₃ cup (105g) honey

Pinch of kosher salt

½ vanilla bean

¼ cup (2oz) finely chopped
   crystallized ginger

Cut the peel and white pith from the grapefruits and then cut the fruit into quarters. Working over a medium bowl separate the grapefruit segments from their membranes, discarding the membranes, pith, and any seeds. Place the fruit in the bowl and tip in any juice pooled on the cutting board.

   Transfer to a food processor and purée until smooth. Return to the bowl. Whisk in the honey and salt, and scrape in the seeds from the vanilla bean. Refrigerate, covered, at least 2 hours.

   Freeze in an ice cream maker according to manufacturers' directions. Transfer it to a freezer-safe container and freeze until desired firmness. Sprinkle with crystallized ginger.

   Tip: Start this sorbet a few hours before you plan to serve it so it has time to firm up.

Pomegranates

Each winter, a pomegranate tree in my neighborhood suddenly fruits. I go out of my way to pass it, marveling at its accomplishment. *Well done*, I whisper. My hope, frankly, is that my words of encouragement will inspire the bobbing ornaments to hang around a little longer. They're just so voluptuous, so immodest as they hang, heavy with juice. I want to throw one to the ground, collect its ink, and paint the sidewalk.

Do the people who own this tree appreciate what they have? Because if it were mine, I would appreciate it. I would appreciate it so much I'd want to share it with everyone. One night, in the wee hours, I'd gather all the pomegranates from my tree and string them from every mailbox and light post in the neighborhood. People would come out in the morning to fetch the newspaper, and . . . surprise!

Tip: The neatest way to release pomegranate seeds (technically *arils*) from their membranes is to quarter each fruit and submerge the pieces in a deep bowl of water. Bend back each section, work the arils free with your fingers, gather them in a strainer, and pick off any white pith. Please, wear an apron.

SIMPLE USES FOR POMEGRANATES:

pomegranate rickey = pomegranate syrup (juice + sugar, boiled) + gin + lime juice + arils

salad = toasted hazelnuts + arugula + orange segments + arils + pomegranate juice + raspberry vinegar + olive oil

breakfast = granola + Greek yogurt + honey + pomegranate arils

Pomegranate Clove Thumbprint Cookies

You know those cookie swaps where everyone tries to outdo everyone else with the fanciest, most design-heavy cookies? And you end up with all manner of dyed royal icing and sticky sweet candied fruits and a sugar high that makes you crazy eyed? These are about 10 billion times better than those cookies.

························· **MAKES 20 COOKIES** ·························

1 cup (120g) whole-wheat flour

½ cup (80g) almond meal

½ teaspoon baking powder

½ teaspoon ground cloves

¼ teaspoon kosher salt

¼ pound (1 stick) butter, at room temperature

⅓ cup plus 1 tablespoon (85g) granulated sugar

1 egg

½ teaspoon almond extract

5 teaspoons pomegranate-raspberry (or plain raspberry) preserves or 100% fruit spread

¼ cup fresh pomegranate arils

In a large bowl, whisk the flour, almond meal, baking powder, cloves, and salt.

In the bowl of a stand mixer, beat the butter on medium-high speed until light and fluffy, about 2 minutes. Stream in the sugar and beat 2 minutes longer, until incorporated. Beat in the egg and almond extract.

With the machine off, dump in the flour mixture. Beat on the lowest speed for 30 seconds, then increase to medium speed and beat just until the dry bits are no longer visible. Refrigerate the dough for at least 1 hour and up to one day.

Preheat the oven to 375°F (190°C). Line 2 rimmed baking sheets with parchment.

Using a 1½-inch (3.75cm) scoop, portion the dough into mounds. With the end of a wooden spoon, drill a deep indentation into each cookie. This will be your "thumbprint." Bake the cookies until completely set and golden brown around the edges, 15 to 18 minutes. Cool completely. (Cookies can be made 2 days ahead and stored, unfilled, in an airtight container.)

Just before serving, fill each thumbprint with ¼ teaspoon preserves and 5 or 6 pomegranate arils.

Radicchio

Radicchio doesn't mess around. It doesn't cajole or soothe, seduce or invite; it stands up tall, squares its shoulders, and dares you to punch it in the gut.

Since you can't really mollify this particular chicory, reset your expectations. Embrace its scarlet color and brash bitterness and use it to your advantage, offsetting sweet citrus, briny olives, salty cheeses, and fruity vinegars. Shred its leaves to boost boring coleslaws, or toss it on the grill to char, turning the vegetable crispy and smoky.

Choose long-leafed Treviso if the more familiar, bocce ball–shaped radicchio, called Chioggia, is too powerful for your delicate sensibilities. Or build up to it slowly, training your palate bit by bit.

Think of radicchio like coffee. The first sip tastes like an ashtray, but soon you'll crave its mojo.

Tip: Radicchio lasts for several days in the fridge, but its bitterness does intensify over time. Enjoy it fresh.

SIMPLE USES FOR RADICCHIO:

grilled radicchio wedges = radicchio quarters + olive oil + sugar + fruity balsamic

pasta = radicchio + sweet onions + pappardelle + fresh ricotta

salad = radicchio + green leaf lettuce + oranges + briny black olives + ricotta salata + raspberry vinaigrette

Radicchio Salad with Tahini Lemon Drizzle

Creamy tahini, tart lemon, mild avocado, and crisp, juicy cucumbers
offset radicchio's bitterness in this big, bold salad. Grab your largest, widest serving bowl.

•• **SERVES 8** ••

½ small head radicchio, cored and
    chopped

1 head butter lettuce, cored and
    chopped

½ unpeeled English cucumber,
    cut in half moons

2 avocados, sliced

2 tablespoons tahini

2 tablespoons extra-virgin olive oil

Juice of 1 lemon (about ¼ cup or
    60ml)

1 garlic clove, minced

½ teaspoon honey

Kosher salt and freshly ground
    black pepper

Toss the chopped radicchio and lettuce in a wide, shallow serving bowl. Scatter the cucumber and avocado on top.

In a medium bowl, whisk the tahini, oil, lemon juice, garlic, honey, ½ teaspoon salt, and ¼ teaspoon pepper. Drizzle the dressing over the salad and serve immediately.

Tip: Should the simplicity of this recipe make you uncomfortable, might I suggest the following complications? A fistful of black olives, a smattering of candied nuts, a sprinkling of croutons—none would be out of place, nor would a plate piled high with warm pita triangles alongside a small bowl of feta cheese.

Radishes

Confession: I have never eaten a French breakfast radish for breakfast.
I don't know who named this particular variety, with its long torso and stringy tail, but I'm guessing it's someone who never had access to almond croissants or Nutella-smeared crêpes. And yet, I readily admit that despite their name, French breakfast radishes are actually quite excellent after 11:59 a.m. Their flavor is mild, and they present with pretty pink tops and cream-colored bottoms. Many of the more common, red-skinned, round radishes look like cherry marbles and taste like pepper balls. This isn't bad per se, so long as you're not expecting gumdrops.

   Whichever variety you choose—and there are many more, including Japanese daikon radishes, which are ivory and tusklike, and watermelon radishes, which look like spin-art—serve them for lunch, dinner, snacks, tea, or whenever normal people finish their breakfast.
Tip: Radishes are exceptionally easy to grow, even for novice gardeners.

SIMPLE USES FOR RADISHES:

hors d'oeuvre = whole French breakfast radishes + fancy French butter + fancy sea salt
creamy salad = sliced radishes + avocado + tomato + garlic buttermilk dressing
tart salad = sliced watermelon radishes + baby spinach + grated green apple +
  cider vinaigrette

Radish Olive Crostini

Serve these fresh, colorful hors d'oeuvres at any outdoor gathering.
Or serve them indoors. Or start serving them outdoors, then move indoors if it rains.
I've given a range for the toppings as baguettes can vary wildly in thickness.

·················· **MAKES ABOUT 18 TOASTS (IF USING A HALF BAGUETTE)**··················
OR 36 (IF USING A FULL BAGUETTE)

½-inch (1.25cm)-thick slices of French baguette

Softened butter

¼ to ½ cup (50g to 80g) pitted Kalamata olives, drained and minced

1 to 2 bunches radishes (French "breakfast" radishes preferred), scrubbed, trimmed, and thinly sliced

1 bunch fresh thyme, leaves only

Zest of 1 lemon

Coarse salt and freshly ground black pepper

Extra-virgin olive oil, for drizzling

Set the broiler rack 4 inches from the heating element.

Lay the bread slices on an ungreased baking sheet. Broil until the edges just turn golden, 1 to 2 minutes, watching carefully. Flip and broil the other side for 30 seconds to 1 minute longer. Cool to room temperature.

Spread each crostini with butter and top with olives and radishes. Sprinkle with thyme leaves, lemon zest, salt, and pepper. Finish with a thin drizzle of olive oil. Serve at room temperature.

Raspberries

In summertime, the temptation to overbuy raspberries is strong. It's not like you won't find a home for the excess. At breakfast, ease them quietly into thick Greek yogurt, setting them down like a pup in a quilt. Or flick them atop granola, splashing them with ice cold milk. Have heavy cream? Whip it into a fluffy, puffy, mousselike frenzy, then drop it from on high. Big creamy snowdrifts will bury those berries so you have to dig around to find them.

Or head down the opposite road, kissing them with heat, dusting them with sugar, and misting them with lemon. Stir once, stir twice, and presto! An eye-popping sauce fit for a poached pear or a humble pancake.

Tip: Store raspberries in a single layer and eat them as fast as possible. Mold waits for no one.

SIMPLE USES FOR RASPBERRIES:

vinaigrette = raspberries + raspberry vinegar + olive oil + shallots
sabayon = yolks + framboise (liqueur) + sugar + cream + raspberries
raspberry ripple ice cream = raspberries + sugar + lemon + vanilla ice cream

Raspberry Melba Sauce

A classic Peach Melba contains raspberry sauce and peaches.
Here, I've worked the peaches right into the sauce. Swap it for the syrup in the Syrupy Nectarine Crêpe Stack (page 96), pour it over coconut ice cream (page 279), or spoon it into Greek yogurt.

· **MAKES 1 TO 1½ CUPS** ·

2 ripe, medium peaches, peeled and diced

2 cups raspberries

¼ cup (63g) granulated sugar

¾ teaspoon lemon juice, or to taste

Combine the peaches, raspberries, sugar, and 3 tablespoons water in a small saucepan over medium-high heat. Bring to a boil. Reduce the heat and let bubble gently until the raspberries fall apart and the peaches are very soft, about 12 minutes, stirring frequently to prevent scorching. Remove from the heat.

If you have an immersion blender, tilt the pan slightly so the sauce pools to one side. Using great caution (the sauce will be very hot), purée with the blender. If you don't have an immersion blender, simply use firmer pressure when straining the sauce in the next step.

Place the sauce in a fine mesh sieve and, using a wooden spoon and some muscle, stir vigorously to force the sauce through the sieve into a medium bowl. Be sure to scrape any sauce that gathers under the strainer into the bowl as well. Discard the seeds. Stir in the lemon juice. Serve warm or cold. (Leftovers may be stored, covered, for several days in the refrigerator.)

Tip: Of course, you could always spoon raspberry sauce on, well, raspberries. I challenge you to deny the universal (though perhaps redundant) appeal of raspberries sauced with themselves.

Red Apples

I once wrote about high antioxidant foods for a well-known magazine. The story highlighted several fruits and vegetables, among them Red Delicious apples, a variety whose skin practically bleeds health-promoting flavonoids.

Do I believe you should now drop everything to go buy Red Delicious apples, claiming you'll sidestep cancer, heart disease, and the sniffles forevermore? Not really. Do I think you should work the peels into places they don't belong (brownies) to neutralize pesky free radicals? Nope. Do I think you should eat them, if you happen to love them? Sure, suit yourself.

But I also personally think—forgive me—that there are far superior red apple varieties out there, among them Fujis, Galas, Braeburns, and countless, no, *thousands* of others. You need to know what you *like*, not just what measures highest on the antioxidant scale.

More than 7,500 apples grow throughout the world, and guess what? They are all good for you.

A McIntosh, for example, tastes quite lovely baked in cider and slopped with cream. Maybe it'll get a slightly lower score on the USDA's ORAC (Oxygen Radical Absorption Capacity) scale, but I'll be too busy enjoying my dessert to care.

Tip: Who says applesauce requires heat? Purée apples raw—cored, seeded, unpeeled—in a food processor with a peeled orange, sugar to taste, and a bit of cinnamon.

SIMPLE USES FOR RED APPLES:

slaw = shredded Cortland apples + carrots + orange juice + red onion + cilantro + pumpkin seeds

breakfast = cooked farro + butter + diced Fuji apples + cashews + cinnamon + brown sugar + milk

snack = small Lady Apples, cored + cottage cheese in the cavity + currants

Cider Baked Apples with Muscovado

I've got nothing against apple pies—in fact, some of my best friends are apple pies—
but skipping the crust is just so much easier. Don't distress if your apples burst their seams.

SERVES 4

4 large McIntosh apples ($1^{3}/_{4}$ to 2 pounds, or 794g to 907g)

2 tablespoons unsalted butter

4 teaspoons dark muscovado sugar, or dark brown sugar

$1/_{2}$ teaspoon ground cinnamon

Kosher salt

$2/_{3}$ cup (158 ml) spiced apple cider

Cold heavy cream, for drizzling

Preheat the oven to 375°F (190°C).

Take a melon baller to each apple and scoop out the stem. Continue scooping, creating a tunnel that reaches about three-quarters of the way down the apple. Discard the seeds and core.

Set the apples in an 8 x 8-inch (20 x 20cm) glass baking dish. Cut 1 tablespoon of the butter into 4 cubes. Drop one cube in each cavity along with 1 teaspoon of muscovado, $1/_{8}$ teaspoon cinnamon, and a pinch of salt. Pour the cider in the bottom of the dish. Plop the remaining tablespoon of butter in the cider and add another pinch of salt.

Bake, uncovered, for 20 minutes. Remove from the oven and baste the apples well, filling their cavities with the liquid. Cover tightly with foil and return to the oven. If you want them to stay intact, remove them after 12 minutes. If you want them extra soft (how I prefer them), leave them in for 3 minutes longer or until the seams burst.

Drizzle each apple with cold heavy cream and, if desired, a bit of the hot, buttery cider.

Red Bell Peppers

If a green bell pepper rang my doorbell, I might look through the peep hole and then pretend I'm not home, easing back from the door so it doesn't see my shadow. But a red bell pepper? That's a different situation. Refreshing and juicy, with a mild, welcome acidity, these crisp vegetables are just as good straight up as they are swept through a clingy dip. Cooking them—on the grill, roasted and blackened over an open flame, or softened in a soup, stew, or the Red Pepper Chili that follows—coaxes out and accentuates their sweetness.

If a red pepper came to the door? I'd let it in, pull out a chair, and invite it to stay. Then I'd tackle it from behind and eat it.

You ring my bell, you take your chances.

Tip: To prep a bell pepper, slice off its top and bottom so you have a smooth pepper tunic. Slit the side and open it flat, then rip out the core and trim out the veins. Now you can slice and dice it with ease.

SIMPLE USES FOR RED BELL PEPPERS:

dip = roasted red peppers + hummus

muhammara = roasted red peppers + walnuts + pomegranate molasses + breadcrumbs + olive oil

ratatouille = red peppers + tomatoes + eggplant + garlic + zucchini + onions + olive oil

Red Pepper Chili

This is, hands down, my go-to winter stew, a red twist on a vegetarian chili I developed
for EatingWell magazine back in 2007. I eat it all season long, either alone
or spooned over Turnip and Yukon Gold Purée (page 303).

•• **SERVES 6** ••

2 tablespoons extra-virgin olive oil

1 large red onion, diced
(about 1¾ cups or 280g)

2 large red bell peppers (about
1 pound or 450g), cut into
1-inch (2.5cm) chunks

5 garlic cloves, minced

2 teaspoons chili powder

1½ teaspoons ground cumin

1 teaspoon dried oregano

Kosher salt and freshly ground
black pepper

2 (15-ounce or 425g) cans kidney
beans, drained and rinsed

2 (14-ounce or 397g) cans diced
tomatoes, undrained

1 to 2 canned chipotle peppers in
adobo sauce, to taste, minced

2 cups (500ml) vegetable stock

2 teaspoons brown sugar

¾ cup (128g) red quinoa, rinsed
well under cool running water

Lime wedges, diced avocado,
cilantro leaves, and sour cream

Heat the oil in a Dutch oven over medium-high heat. Add the onion, bell peppers, garlic, chili powder, cumin, oregano, and ½ teaspoon each salt and pepper. Cook, stirring occasionally, until tender, about 5 minutes. Add the beans, tomatoes with juice, chipotle peppers, stock, and brown sugar. Bring to a boil, reduce heat, and simmer, covered, for 25 minutes.

Stir in the quinoa, cover, and cook over low heat for 15 minutes longer. Remove from the heat. Let stand, covered, for 20 minutes, to thicken. Serve with limes, avocado, cilantro, and sour cream.

Tip: The chili will thicken further as it cools.

Rhubarb

If you want to live long enough to down the Rhubarb Cherry Mini Crisps on page 56, don't eat rhubarb leaves. They are—how do you say?—poisonous. You might think the stalks were toxic, too, if you tasted them raw, but they're not. Their intense sourness simply needs to be tempered with some heat and a generous fistful of sugar.

Hailing from China, rhubarb—technically a vegetable though widely consumed as a fruit—was once prized for its medicinal properties. Later, new varieties were cultivated for use in pies and tarts, earning this confusing but beloved vegetable a most estimable nickname: Pie Plant.

Bakers appreciate how beautifully it melds with strawberries, raspberries, apples, and cherries. I prize its demure, blush-toned hue and the way it turns jammy and glossy as it stews. It's my favorite sugar-it-up-then-bake-it-in-a-pie-vegetable-with-poisonous-leaves, by far.

Tip: Rhubarb freezes well. Grab an extra bunch of stalks, chunk them up, and then freeze them flat on a lined baking sheet. Transfer to a freezer-safe bag.

SIMPLE USES FOR RHUBARB:

cobbler = strawberries + rhubarb + sugar + cornstarch + lemon + butter + flour + baking powder + egg

jam = raspberries + rhubarb + sugar + lemon

rhubarb rice pudding = rhubarb + rice + water + sugar + vanilla + milk

Rhubarb Cherry Mini Crisps

These individual crisps made in shallow crème brûlée molds create a dazzling display of color, texture, and flavor. Add an additional tablespoon of sugar to the rhubarb if you prefer a sweeter filling.

·· SERVES 4 ··

4 tablespoons cold, unsalted butter, cut into 6 pieces, plus soft butter for greasing the baking dishes

1 pound rhubarb, ends trimmed and stalks sliced crosswise $1/4$ inch (0.65cm) thick

$1/2$ pound (227g) dark red cherries, stemmed and pitted (about $1\frac{1}{4}$ cups)

2 tablespoons granulated sugar

$1/2$ teaspoon balsamic vinegar

$1/2$ cup (100g) packed light brown sugar

$1/3$ cup (42g) all-purpose flour

$1/2$ cup (45g) old-fashioned rolled oats

$1/4$ teaspoon ground cinnamon

$1/8$ teaspoon kosher salt

$1/4$ cup (35g) pine nuts, toasted, optional

$1/4$ cup to $1/2$ cup (60 to 120ml) cold heavy cream, for serving

Preheat the oven to 375°F (190°C). Smear a bit of soft butter inside four 8-ounce (227g) crème brûlée dishes and set on a rimmed baking sheet.

In a large bowl, combine the rhubarb, cherries, granulated sugar, and vinegar. Toss well.

In a food processor fitted with the metal blade, combine the cold butter, brown sugar, flour, oats, cinnamon, and salt. Pulse about 35 to 40 times, in short bursts, until the mixture just begins to clump. Transfer to a small bowl. Stir in the pine nuts.

Pack 1 cup of the fruit into each baking dish. (Mound it high.) Divide the topping among the dishes and press to adhere. Bake in the upper third of the oven until the fruit bubbles vigorously and the topping is deep brown, 35 to 40 minutes. Cool for at least 10 minutes.

Serve warm, cold, or at room temperature, drizzled generously with cream.

Tip: I love the crunch of pine nuts in this recipe, but feel free to leave them out.

Strawberries

Years ago, as a newly minted culinary school graduate, I felt pretty special. Suddenly, I could slice, I could dice, I could fix a broken hollandaise. You want me to tie up your crêpe with a chive? Watch me. I'll do it one handed, with my eyes closed, under water.

Fast-forward two days.

I was working at a bakery and the owner, who never liked me, set three flats of strawberries on my table. "Slice them."

So I did. I took the paring knife, carefully sliced the stem from each berry, and made perfect, even slivers. I sliced, and I sliced, and I sliced. I was pretty proud of myself, actually. The strawberries were coming along nicely.

The owner approached. "You finished?"

I showed her the eight strawberries, beaming. Check me out, sister!

"You're not too quick with the knife," she hissed, yanking the blade from my hand. In about 35 seconds, she finished the three flats—that's 36 pounds—herself.

I wasn't long for that bakery.

But I did learn a few things while there. One, I slice slowly, but I type quickly. Two, I don't like being yelled at. Three, the best way to prep strawberries isn't to slice them at all. It's to grab them whole, by the stems, and sink them in chocolate.

Tip: It's easier to hull strawberries with a knife than with a fancy strawberry huller. Spend your money on something else.

SIMPLE USES FOR STRAWBERRIES:

breakfast = crêpes + strawberries + mascarpone + vanilla + orange
dessert = pavlova + Grand Marnier macerated strawberries
salad = dandelion greens + strawberries + almonds + balsamic

White and Dark Chocolate Strawberries

I served these strawberries at a large potluck and plopped them on a table
laden with tarts, pies, cookies, and brownies. The strawberries disappeared first.

·············· **MAKES 40 TO 45 STRAWBERRIES (RECIPE MAY BE SCALED UP OR DOWN)** ···········

8 ounces (227g) good quality dark chocolate, chopped

2 pounds (907g) impeccably fresh medium to large strawberries (35 to 45), rinsed and pat dry

4 ounces (113g) good quality white chocolate, chopped

Line two rimmed baking sheets with silicone liners or wax paper.

Melt the dark chocolate in a heatproof bowl set over a saucepan of barely simmering water, stirring occasionally, until completely smooth, about 5 minutes. Remove the bowl from the heat and wipe the underside dry with a tea towel. To make dipping easier, scrape the chocolate into a smaller bowl.

Hold each strawberry by its stem. Dip it into the chocolate about three-quarters of the way up the berry. Drag it against the side of the bowl to stop any drips, then transfer to the baking sheet. Repeat with the remaining strawberries. Pop the baking sheets into the refrigerator for 15 minutes to set the chocolate.

Meanwhile, set the white chocolate in a second heatproof bowl (or wash and dry the first bowl) and melt over simmering water as you did with the dark chocolate. Set a quart-size zip-top bag in a drinking glass. Open it so the edges reach halfway down the sides of the glass. Scrape the melted white chocolate into the bag. Seal the bag, pressing out any air as you zip it shut.

Remove the strawberries from the fridge and condense them onto a single baking sheet. Snip off the tiniest corner of the zip-top bag, squeeze gently, and wave your wrist quickly side to side so the chocolate drizzles haphazardly over the berries. (You may have a bit of white chocolate left over.)

Set the berries back in the fridge for 5 minutes and serve.

Tip: Choose berries with impeccably smooth leaves. Shriveled or otherwise sad leaves ruin the visual impact of this lovely dessert.

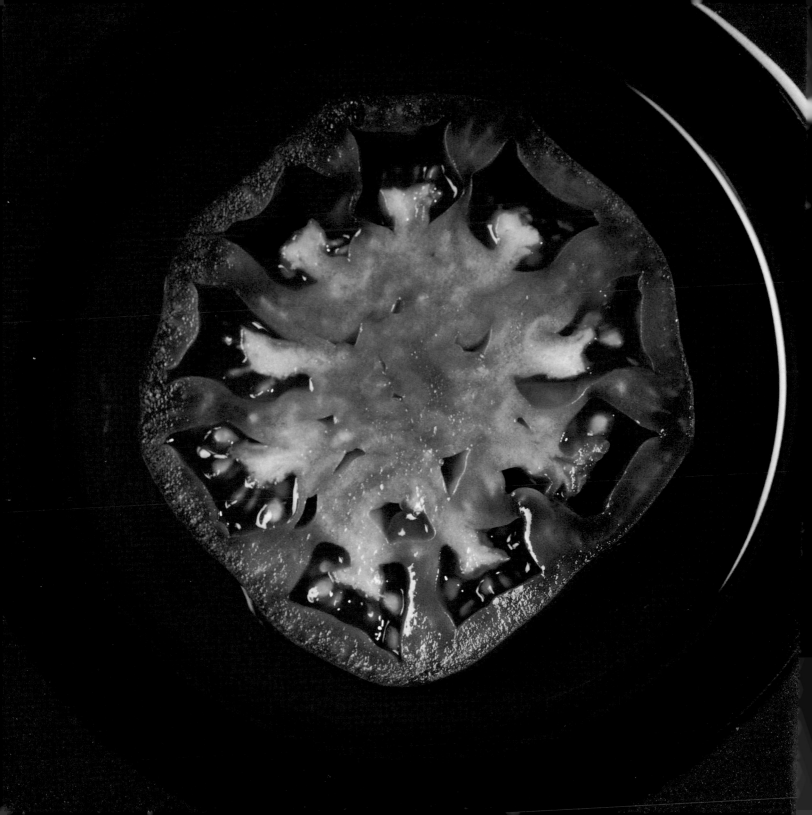

Tomatoes

In her book *More Home Cooking: A Writer Returns to the Kitchen*, beloved food writer Laurie Colwin compared a world without tomatoes to a string quartet without violins. I would modify Colwin's analogy by adding the word *good*. A world without good tomatoes is like a string quartet without violins. For anyone who has ever been crossed by a hard, mealy, cold, or otherwise offensive tomato would probably rather eat a violin than that tomato.

But beautiful summer tomatoes, warm and juicy from the vine, rubbed on hard bread, sprinkled with salt, tickled with balsamic, that, my friends, is a pleasure tomatophiles wait all year for. We hold our collective breath for the moment we can finally exhale and release our pent-up anticipation. Then we grab a sharp knife, make a quick cut, and watch the juices pool on our cutting boards.

Tip: Never store uncut tomatoes in the refrigerator. Case closed.

SIMPLE USES FOR TOMATOES:

basic tomato sauce = plum tomatoes + garlic + basil + olive oil + tomato paste

panzanella = stale olive bread + tomatoes + corn + cucumbers + red onions + olive vinaigrette

gazpacho = tomatoes + red onions + bell peppers + cucumber + olive oil + red wine vinegar + garlic + tomato juice

Open-Faced Smoky Tomato Grilled Cheese

A ripe summer tomato crowned with smoky, gooey cheese elevates this comfort food
classic to another realm entirely. Pairing it with a green salad is a must.

························· **SERVES 4** ·························

½ pound (227g) smoked mozzarella, wrapped in foil, frozen
for 10 minutes

4 slices thick-cut country-style,
sourdough, or pugliese bread

1 tablespoon extra-virgin olive oil,
plus additional for drizzling

1 large or 2 medium beefsteak
tomatoes, cut into 4 thick slices

4 sprigs basil, for garnish

Lightly dressed salad greens, for
serving

Set the broiler rack 5 inches from the heat source.

Shred the cheese on the largest holes of a box grater. You'll have 3 scant cups.

Place the bread on a rimmed baking sheet. Brush both sides with the oil. Broil on one side for 1 minute only, or until the top feels just slightly toasted but is not yet colored. Remove from the oven (keep the broiler on) and flip the bread.

Lay 1 thick tomato slice on each piece of bread. Divide the cheese among the bread slices, pressing firmly so it adheres and blankets the bread's entire surface. (If some falls on the sheet pan, let it. It makes a crispy and delicious garnish.)

Return to the broiler until the cheese bubbles and turns golden brown, watching carefully and snatching the pan from the oven just before it burns. Drizzle each slice with a thin stream of olive oil, garnish with a basil sprig, and serve with plenty of salad.

Tip: Because each sandwich has a whopping ¾ cup of cheese, serve only one slice per person.

Watermelon

On a scorching August day, when the sun melts your skin and the sweat pours like rain, slice a hunk of ripe, red watermelon and settle under a tree. No iPod, no children, no to-dos. Silence your internal rambling, ignore more pressing concerns, and prepare to ruin your shirt. Chances are, you have others, and this one's not so great anyway. Now stop thinking about your shirt. Watermelons are best consumed with abandon, while fully present, when ready to let go. You can't eat them demurely, so why bother trying? Spit the seeds hard, like you mean it; now spit them harder.

It's summer, and no matter how much you'd like it to, it will not, it cannot, last forever.

Tip: Personal-sized watermelons now share market space with more traditional, bathtub-sized varieties. Whichever you favor, make sure it's heavy for its size.

SIMPLE USES FOR WATERMELON:

grilled watermelon = watermelon + hot grill

salad = watermelon + cucumber + chiles + mint leaves

popsicles = puréed watermelon + paper cups + craft sticks

Watermelon Slushie

When it's crazy hot, we all crave something *refreshing that's not too sweet. This icy cooler is like popping a straw in a watermelon and drinking it, only slightly easier.*

SERVES 3 OR 4

2 pound hunk of seedless watermelon (rind-on weight)

Juice of 1 lime (2½ tablespoons juice)

⅓ cup plus 1 tablespoon (79ml) water

3 leaves fresh mint, chopped,
  plus additional mint sprigs, for garnish

1 tablespoon granulated sugar

Line a baking sheet with parchment, wax paper, or a silicone liner.

Cut the melon into thick slices. Remove and discard the rind, then cut the flesh into rough, ice-cube size chunks. (You should have about 1½ pounds, 680g, of chunks.) Place in a single layer on the lined baking sheet. Freeze for exactly 30 minutes. (Some snowy freezer burn may appear. Ignore it.)

Pop the frozen watermelon cubes into a food processor or ice-crushing blender along with the lime juice, water, chopped mint, and sugar. Whirl for 1 minute. Stop the machine, scrape down the sides, and process for a few seconds longer, or until the drink is thick and frosty, with no chunks remaining. Serve immediately, garnished with additional mint sprigs, if desired.

ORANGE

Apricots

Raise a ripe apricot to your nose and breathe in deeply. Tell me you don't smell summer screeching round the bend.

Prized for their luscious flesh, velvety skin, and sun-drenched color, apricots once dominated what's now called Silicon Valley, home today to Google, Yahoo, Facebook, and me. And though the epicenter of apricot production has shifted a bit southeastward, the Golden State still produces roughly 95 percent of the domestic crop.

Most of us are familiar with pale yellow to deep orange apricots, but Middle Eastern varieties can be pink, white, gray, or even black. In fact, Turkey and Iran top the list of nations that grow an estimated six billion pounds of apricots worldwide. Cultivation actually dates back several millennia, to northeastern China, as early 2000 B.C.

That's even older than my shoes, and I haven't bought new shoes in a very, very long time. *Tip:* Dried apricots, per serving, actually have significantly more fiber than fresh ones and twice the potassium of a banana. So while you should definitely go crazy with fresh apricots during their short seasonal peak, opt for dried the rest of the year.

SIMPLE USES FOR APRICOTS:

dessert = grilled apricots + melted chocolate + toasted pistachios + cold heavy cream
snack = fresh apricots + whole milk ricotta + honey + crushed almonds
brunch = poached fresh or dried apricots + crêpes + crème fraîche + cherries

Apricot Frangipane Galette

With a tender crust, sweet-tart apricots, and creamy almond filling,
this rustic galette is my take on a classic French dessert.

·················· SERVES 6 TO 8 ··················

For the crust:

1 cup plus 1 tablespoon (128g) all-purpose flour

¼ cup (40g) almond meal

¼ teaspoon kosher salt

1 tablespoon sugar

9 tablespoons cold butter, cut into tablespoons

¾ teaspoon almond extract

2 tablespoons ice water

For the almond frangipane:

½ cup (80g) almond meal

¼ cup (63g) sugar

4 tablespoons butter, at room temperature

1 egg, separated

½ teaspoon almond extract

Pinch of kosher salt

For the fruit:

4 to 5 apricots (about 10 ounces), pitted and quartered

1 tablespoon sugar

½ teaspoon lemon juice

Make the crust: In the bowl of a stand mixer fitted with the paddle attachment, mix the flour, almond meal, salt, sugar, and cold butter on low speed until clumps begin to form, about 1 minute. Add the almond extract and ice water and continue mixing until the dough comes together in a mass, 1 to 2 minutes. Transfer to a large sheet of plastic wrap, flatten into a $4\frac{1}{2}$-inch (11.5 cm) disc, wrap tightly, and refrigerate for 1 hour.

Meanwhile, make the frangipane: Beat the almond meal, sugar, butter, egg yolk (reserve the egg white), almond extract, and salt on medium speed in the same mixing bowl until smooth, about 1 minute. Refrigerate, covered, until the crust is ready.

Line a heavy rimmed baking sheet with parchment. In a large bowl, toss the apricots with the sugar and lemon juice. On a floured countertop, roll out the chilled dough to a rough 11-inch (28cm) circle. Transfer to the prepared baking sheet. Spread the frangipane thickly over the dough, leaving a $1\frac{1}{2}$-inch (4cm) border. Scatter the apricots cut-sides up atop the frangipane, scraping any juices on top. (Do not pile the apricots in a heap. If they don't fit, eat them separately.) Fold in the pastry, pleating as you go, leaving a 4 to 5 inch (10 to 13cm) circle of fruit exposed. Freeze on the baking sheet for 20 minutes.

Meanwhile, preheat the oven to 450°F (230°C). Whisk the reserved egg white until frothy. Brush it on the exposed pastry. Bake in the center of the oven for 25 to 30 minutes, or until the pastry is golden brown and the frangipane is set. Transfer the baking sheet to a cooling rack. Allow the galette to cool to room temperature, at least 30 minutes. Because the pastry is exremely delicate, slice and serve directly from the baking sheet.

Butternut Squash

Picking one's favorite squash is like picking one's favorite child, only harder. This one's so quirky, but that one's so pretty! This one's so versatile, but that one's big enough to hold six quarts of stew! And so on.

Eventually, for this book, I narrowed it down to sugar pie pumpkins (see page 109) and butternuts. Somewhere, a delicata weeps.

Butternuts charm me not only because their name evokes Life Savers (butternut rum, the best flavor ever), but because you can take them in a million directions. Grate them raw, purée them in soups, roast thick wedges, or bake until tender enough to scoop with a spoon. Butternuts skate on the sweet side, so you can either play this up or introduce contrasting spice and heat.

Do experiment, and please, go buy a heavy knife. You'll need it.

Tip: Peeling a raw butternut is a chore. Instead, try halving or quartering the unpeeled squash and roasting it until tender. Then scoop out the flesh and chop or purée.

SIMPLE USES FOR BUTTERNUT SQUASH:

warm grain salad = roasted squash + wild rice + dried cranberries + toasted hazelnuts + cranberry-hazelnut vinaigrette

soup = squash + butter + onion + stock + coriander + spicy pepitas + sour cream + cilantro

pasta = penne + squash + brown butter + sage + breadcrumbs

Red Curry Glazed Butternut Squash with Coconut Rice

Love butternut squash but don't love peeling it? This pair of compatible sides is for you. Look for Thai red curry paste near the coconut milk in your supermarket.

························· **SERVES 4 AS A SIDE** ·························

2 teaspoons Thai red curry paste

1 teaspoon honey

1 cup plus 1 teaspoon (237ml) light coconut milk, divided

1 (2-pound or 907g) butternut squash, unpeeled, stem sliced off

1 tablespoon extra-virgin olive oil

Kosher salt and freshly ground black pepper

1½ cups (250g) rice (brown or white)

Pinch sugar

About 15 plucked cilantro leaves

Toasted cashews, unsweetened toasted coconut, and/or toasted sesame seeds, for garnish

Preheat the oven to 450°F (230°C) with a rack in the upper third position.

In a small bowl, whisk the red curry paste, honey, and 1 teaspoon of the coconut milk until smooth.

Halve the squash lengthwise, scrape out the seeds and strings, and halve lengthwise again to form four long quarters. Set face up on a rimmed baking sheet. Drizzle with the olive oil and sprinkle generously with salt and pepper, rubbing to coat. Knock the pieces on their sides.

Roast for 20 minutes, or until the undersides are nicely browned. Flip onto their other sides and roast 10 minutes longer.

Meanwhile, in a medium saucepan, combine the rice, the remaining 1 cup of coconut milk, 1 cup water, sugar, and ¼ teaspoon salt. Bring to a boil, reduce heat, cover, and simmer gently until the liquid is absorbed and the rice is tender. Remove from the heat, keeping covered. (Alternatively, use a rice cooker.)

When the squash is ready, remove it from the oven and switch on the broiler.

Brush the squash thickly with the red curry mixture. Broil face up until the paste bubbles and darkens, watching carefully, about 2 minutes. Serve the squash and rice in shallow bowls (with spoons), sprinkling with the cilantro and your choice of additional garnishes.

Tip: For a complete meal, serve beans, tofu, or lentils alongside.

Carrots

If vegetables earned stars for versatility, carrots would glow like a constellation. Sweet and crunchy raw, they also take beautifully to pickling, puréeing, roasting, glazing, braising, and spicing. But there's one preparation method I still can't get behind: boiling. A boiled carrot is a travesty.

When I was growing up, my best friend's parents had a rule: eat your vegetables, or no dessert. One night when I stayed over for dinner, they served boiled carrots. Too young to flee their house, and too prissy to flaunt their rules, I suffered those carrots for two measly Oreos, a dessert so inadequate it redefined what I considered injustice.

Today, I eat carrots all the time. The crisper always has a bunch, if not two, at the ready for velvety soups or crunchy slaws. And if I ever invest in a high-octane juicer, it will be to indulge my singular passion for carrot-orange juice, a drink so good it almost erases the lingering sting of that ill-fated night, a night I abandoned my convictions for two store-bought cookies.

Tip: When buying carrots at the farmers' market, ask the vendor to twist off the frilly tops. They'll take up less space in the fridge and won't suffer from the violence.

SIMPLE USES FOR CARROTS:

salad = wide carrot ribbons + harissa + yogurt + green olives + parsley
sauté = carrot coins + butter + maple syrup + coriander
pickled = carrot sticks + cider vinegar + garlic + water + sugar + salt + crushed red pepper

Carrot Soup with Garam Masala Cream

Here's a creamy soup with a gentle kick from the spice mix garam masala,
a warming combo of coriander, cumin, cinnamon, clove, pepper, bay,
and several other spices. You'll find it in any Indian market.

·· **SERVES 6** ··

1/4 cup (60ml) olive oil

3/4 cup (120g) diced yellow onion

4 to 6 medium carrots (about 1 1/2 pounds, or 680g), peeled, quartered lengthwise, and roughly chopped

1 small yam (about 7 ounces, or 198g), peeled and diced

Kosher salt and freshly ground black pepper

3/4 teaspoon garam masala, divided

3 cups (725ml) vegetable stock

2 teaspoons fresh lime juice, or to taste

2 tablespoons sour cream, plus additional for garnish

Heat the oil in a large soup pot over medium heat. Add the onion, carrots, yam, 1 teaspoon salt, 1/4 teaspoon pepper, and 1/2 teaspoon of the garam masala. Cook for about 15 minutes, stirring frequently.

Add the stock and 1 cup cold water and raise the heat to high. Bring the soup to a boil, then reduce the heat to a simmer, partially cover, and simmer until the vegetables are tender, about 15 minutes. Remove from the heat.

If you have an immersion blender, use it to purée the soup. (Otherwise, allow it to cool slightly and then purée it in batches using a traditional blender. Return the soup to the pot.) Season with the lime juice, to taste, and adjust the salt and pepper.

Mix the sour cream and the remaining 1/4 teaspoon garam masala in a small bowl. Swirl into the soup. Serve hot, garnished with additional sour cream, if desired.

Clementines

Little kid fingers can do many things, but peeling oranges can be tricky. Happily, we have clementines, a super-sweet mandarin variety anyone with opposable thumbs can unzip and eat. Open a sheet of newspaper, toss your kids some clementines, and go about your day. So long as they're beyond choking age, you won't have much to worry about, unless they can read the day's headlines and the news isn't good.

Better yet, buy a five-pound crate of these small, friendly fruits and set it on the table. I'd wager five bucks that by day's end someone, maybe you?, will feel an inexplicable urge to build a pyramid.

When you're done horsing around and tire of picking them up from the floor, transfer the crate to the fridge and get yourself a glass of wine. You've worked hard enough.

Tip: Like other citrus fruits, clementines have plenty of vitamin C. Combine them with iron-rich foods to improve its absorption.

SIMPLE USES FOR CLEMENTINES:

side = clementines + stock-cooked couscous + capers + pine nuts + chickpeas + shallots
basic salad = clementines + baby spinach + kidney beans + red wine vinaigrette
sophisticated salad = clementines + Belgian (red) endive + black olives + clementine vinaigrette

Clementine Creamsicle Milk Shakes

Creamsicles, those frozen orange Popsicles with the cream-filled center,
were wildly popular when I was a kid, but they were filled with questionable ingredients.
Now you can make your own in drinkable form.

SERVES 2 (MAY BE EASILY DOUBLED)

1 cup (76g) vanilla ice cream

2 clementines, peeled, strings and
as much clingy white pith removed as possible

½ cup (120ml) milk

Combine the ice cream, clementines, and milk in a blender and blend
until frothy and completely smooth, 1 to 2 minutes. Serve.

Kumquats

Brace yourself, for if there is one member of the citrus kingdom that is not at all what it seems, it's the cute and perky kumquat, a fruit no bigger than a swollen tonsil. Pop it in your mouth whole, bite down on the mild rind, and then hold onto something sturdy.

The juice is tart.

For those who favor the yin and yang of foods that contain their polar opposites (think salted caramels), kumquats make an ideal snack. And though your first bite may shock you, you will soon find the sweet-tart fruit tough to quit.

In fact, I tried my first kumquat about two years ago, and except for an occasional break to sleep, feed my children, and wait for winter to bring kumquats back in season, I've been eating them pretty much ever since.

Tip: Because you eat the rind, seek out organic kumquats whenever possible. Be prepared to spit out larger seeds.

SIMPLE USES FOR KUMQUATS:

snack = whole kumquats + deglet noor dates (alternate one then the other)
kumquat sidecar = cognac + orange liqueur + kumquats + ice + sugared rim
dessert = poached kumquats (in sugar + water + vanilla) + poppy seeds + crème fraiche

Kumquat Arugula Salad with Currant-Walnut Vinaigrette

Here's a salad that hits multiple flavor notes, from sharp and acidic to sweet and toasty. Don't be put off by the dressing's initial appearance. Once tossed through the salad, its seductive flavor, and the beauty of the salad as a whole, will win you right over.

···················· SERVES 2 AS A LARGE LUNCH ENTRÉE, OR 4 AS A SIDE SALAD ····················

¼ cup (1.3oz) dried currants

15 kumquats, divided

3 cups packed (3oz) baby arugula

½ cup walnut halves (about 1½oz), toasted

⅓ cup (79ml) walnut oil

¼ teaspoon red wine vinegar

Kosher salt and freshly ground black pepper

Set the currants in a small bowl or ramekin. Cover with about ½ cup boiling water. Plump for 5 minutes. Drain.

Slice 10 of the kumquats into thin rounds, discarding any seeds. Add to a large salad bowl. Scatter in the arugula, walnuts, and half the currants.

Roughly chop the remaining 5 kumquats, discarding their seeds, and place them in a mini food processor along with the remaining currants. Pulse to mince. Add the walnut oil, vinegar, ¼ teaspoon salt, and ⅛ teaspoon pepper, and purée until you have an emulsified dressing, about 1 minute. (Tiny bits of fruit will remain visible.) Adjust seasonings to taste.

Pour half of the vinaigrette over the salad and toss gently with tongs. Divide among serving plates, and finish with coarse salt and cracked pepper. Pass the remaining vinaigrette alongside.

Tip: To toast walnuts, bake in a preheated 350°F (175°C) oven until golden, 4 to 6 minutes, stirring once.

Mangoes

Mangoes fall into several camps, including those that are strawberry and lime colored and shaped like overgrown beans (the Tommy Atkins variety, for example), those that are banana-colored (like the Ataulfo), and countless others too many to list. Mango aficionados like my friend Denise Marchessault, a Le Cordon Bleu–trained pastry chef and cooking school owner from Victoria, British Columbia, strongly prefers what she unequivocally calls the "superior" Ataulfo. Praising them as incredibly sweet and aromatic, she hails their flesh as creamy smooth, and appreciates how much less fibrous and stringy they are than other varieties. This sounds like discrimination to me, but I just work here.

Tip: Picture a soapy baby. Now prevent this baby from wiggling. Isn't that fun? Handling a peeled mango approximates this challenge, so it's generally easier to prep it with the peel still on. To do this, stand the mango at attention. Run a heavy knife downward, just right of center, curving snugly around the large central seed. Repeat on the other side. These rounded sections are sometimes called mango "cheeks," and you can crosshatch them with a paring knife and then slice the cubes right off. If you simply want to eat the mango, invert the cheeks, thrust them towards your mouth, and nuzzle the dice with a gentle but thorough kiss.

SIMPLE USES FOR MANGOES:

salsa = diced mango + diced jicama + red chile + avocado + lime + cilantro
lassi = mango + yogurt + milk + sugar + cardamom
traditional Thai dessert = mango + coconut milk + sugar + sticky rice

Mangoes with Lime Crème Anglaise

This vibrant, tropical recipe was generously provided by my dear friend Denise Marchessault,
who runs the intimate and quite phenomenal cooking school French Mint out of her picturesque
home in Victoria. The smaller you dice your fruit, the prettier this dessert will be.

.... SERVES 4 TO 6 ....

Crème anglaise:

1 cup (237ml) whole milk

¼ cup plus 1 tablespoon (64g)
   granulated sugar

3 egg yolks

2 tablespoons fresh lime juice, plus
   more, to taste (from 1 lime)

Fruit:

2 small Ataulfo mangoes, peeled,
   cut into ¼-inch (0.65cm) dice

1 cup diced fresh pineapple, cut
   into ¼ inch dice

Fresh mint and raspberries, for
   garnish (optional)

To make the sauce: In a medium saucepan, stir the milk with half the sugar. Bring to a boil and remove from the heat. In a small bowl, whisk the yolks with the remaining sugar. Whisk a bit of the hot milk mixture into the yolks, then scrape back into the saucepan. Gently cook over medium heat, whisking constantly. Do not let boil. The sauce is ready when it lightly coats the back of a spoon.

Stir in 2 tablespoons of the lime juice. Taste, and add a bit more, 1 teaspoon at a time, if you prefer a more pronounced lime flavor. Strain through a fine-mesh sieve into a clean bowl. Cool to room temperature, then refrigerate, covered, until cold. (The sauce may be made up to two days in advance.)

To assemble: Combine the mango and pineapple in a bowl. Drizzle with some crème anglaise and toss to coat. Spoon into pretty dessert glasses. Alternately, place a 2⅞-inch (7.5cm) round cookie cutter on a small serving plate. Pack it with the mango and pineapple, then slowly lift up the cutter. Repeat with the remaining fruit. In either case, garnish each portion with mint and fresh raspberries, if desired.

Nectarines

No one's claiming that peaches don't deserve their hallowed place in summer fruit lore, but can we please give it up for nectarines? Presenting in both yellow- and white-fleshed varieties, nectarines provide all the benefits of a peach without the fuzzy skin. Eating one is like kissing a baby's cheek, instead of the cheek of a teenage boy who hasn't quite started shaving yet but who, let's face it, probably should.

Perhaps there's no point in maligning a peach to build up a nectarine: both fruits have plenty to offer and similar culinary applications. Toss nectarines in smoothies or scones (try pairing them with ginger), scoop ice cream in their tender hollows, or pack some in a picnic basket with arugula, goat cheese, and French bread.

Best of all, nectarines don't ever have to be peeled. Take that, peach.

Tip: To pit a ripe but firm nectarine, slice it in a big circle from pole to pole, then twist the halves apart in opposite directions. If the fruit is too soft for this technique, cut out wedges with a small paring knife instead, discarding the pit as the last step.

SIMPLE USES FOR NECTARINES:

relish = diced nectarines + cherries + red onion + ginger
dessert = grilled nectarines + tart frozen yogurt + crushed Amaretti cookies
shake = nectarines + blueberries + frozen banana chunks + flaxseed + soy milk

Syrupy Nectarine Crêpe Stack

Drumroll, please: this tall stack of crêpes heaped with fresh, sweet nectarines
makes quite an entrance. Serve on the weekend for a special family breakfast.

························ **SERVES 4** ························

2 nectarines, pitted and thinly
   sliced (see Tip on page 95)

3 tablespoons maple syrup

3½ tablespoons melted butter,
   cooled slightly, divided

½ cup (63g) all-purpose flour

½ cup (118ml) milk (not fat free)

2 eggs

2 teaspoons brandy, optional

Kosher salt

Greek yogurt, for garnish

Toss the nectarines and syrup in a medium bowl. Set aside.

In a blender, whiz 2 tablespoons of the melted butter, the flour, milk, eggs, brandy (if using), pinch of salt, and 2 tablespoons water until smooth. Transfer to a pitcher or a lipped measuring cup.

Heat an 8½-inch (21.5cm) nonstick skillet over medium-high heat until drops of water sizzle. Brush the bottom and sides of the skillet with a bit of the melted butter. Tilt the pan forward, then pour about 2½ table-spoons of the batter into the lip of the pan. Quickly swirl so the batter coats the bottom of the skillet. Cook until the underside is lacy and the edges look dry, 30 to 45 seconds. Flip and cook for 15 to 30 seconds longer. Transfer to a dinner plate. Repeat with the remaining batter, slick-ing the pan with a thin coating of melted butter between each crêpe. Stack the crêpes, about 10 total.

To serve, spoon the syrupy nectarine slices over the top of the crêpe stack. Cut the stack in quarters, and serve 1 tall quarter per person, spooning any fallen nectarines on top and alongside each serving. Gar-nish with Greek yogurt.

Tip: The batter may be made one day in advance. Or, you may make the crêpes one day in advance and stack them on a large plate, covered, in the refrigerator. Microwave the stack, covered with a paper towel, for 1 minute before topping with the syrupy nectarines and yogurt.

Papayas

With creamy flesh that ranges from orange to yellow to white, papayas enjoy worldwide popularity, especially in Latin America and tropical regions, where vendors may slice one up and hand you a wedge on the spot.

Spritz ripe papaya with lime, or blend it with bananas and grab a straw. You can also try classic Thai *som tum*, a shredded green papaya salad that showcases the fruit in its unripe state. In true Thai style, this dish hits four flavor notes—sour, hot, salty, and sweet—simultaneously. (Note: *Som tum* contains fish sauce and sometimes shellfish, so vegetarians be warned.)

Whatever you do, don't drop a papaya in your kitchen. Its seeds are many, and if your luck is like mine, they'll find their way underneath your refrigerator, a place, I'm guessing, you'd rather leave unexplored.

Tip: Papaya seeds may either be discarded or blended into dressings, a popular way to showcase their peppery flavor.

SIMPLE USES FOR PAPAYAS:

dessert = ripe papaya + coconut ice cream

snack = roasted papaya + lime + salt + chili powder or cayenne pepper

fruit salad = papaya + honeydew + cantaloupe + mango + pineapple

Quick Papaya Smoothie

Papaya shines in a pretty morning smoothie that's both creamy and dairy free. (The frozen banana adds body.) Coconut water lends a subtle flavor but keeps the texture nice and light, though you should feel free to substitute another liquid of your choice. Pineapple, orange, or pomegranate juices would certainly get the job done, too.

SERVES 2

½ large or one small ripe banana, cut in chunks, frozen until hard

½ cup (112g) frozen, pitted dark sweet cherries

½ small Mexican or other orange-fleshed papaya (about 1 pound or 454g), peeled, seeded, and cubed

½ cup (118ml) coconut water

1 tablespoon ground flaxseed, optional

Combine the banana, cherries, papaya, coconut water, and flaxseed, if using, in a blender. Purée until smooth. Serve immediately.

Tip: Coconut water—the liquid from inside a fresh coconut (see page 278)—is now more widely available than ever. Look for it in shelf-stable cartons in the juice aisle.

Peaches

Peaches have their own license plates (Georgia), their own Roald Dahl book (*James and the Giant Peach*), their own retro music duo (Peaches & Herb), and their own *Beverly Hills 90210* hangout (The Peach Pit).

They've also been honored in poet-author David Mas Masumoto's *Epitaph for a Peach,* a moving reflection on his family's Del Rey, California, peach and grape farm.

Of course, for all their literary and cultural import, peaches also make swell eating. Top slices with soft chèvre, chop them up for crisps and crumbles, brandy them, grill them, roast them, or simply dribble them with cold, heavy cream. Peaches *are* summer, juicy and sweet, a season, captured, for all to enjoy.

Tip: To remove the skin of a peach, make an X in the bottom of the fruit with a small paring knife. Plunge the peaches into rapidly boiling water for 45 seconds, then transfer to ice water. The skin will lift right off. (Firmer peaches can often be peeled raw with a vegetable peeler.)

SIMPLE USES FOR PEACHES:

parfait = peaches + ginger simple syrup + mascarpone + sweetened ricotta + crystallized ginger

chutney = peaches + sugar + white wine vinegar + cloves + allspice

bellini = peach nectar + Prosecco or Champagne

Peach Mascarpone Flatbreads

Here's a hearty hors d'oeuvre best suited to a picnic, barbecue, or pool party rather than an elegant, pinkie-out affair. In other words, this dish is generously portioned. Eat it with gusto, and use a plate. Finally, keep in mind that prepared flatbreads come in all shapes and sizes, so the quantities of the remaining ingredients may fluctuate depending on how much surface area you're working with.

•••••••••••••••••••••••••••••••• **SERVES 4 TO 6 AS AN APPETIZER** ••••••••••••••••••••••••••••••••

1 orange

4 whole-wheat flatbreads

2 tablespoons extra-virgin olive oil

Kosher salt and freshly ground black pepper

½ cup (4 ounces or 113g) mascarpone cheese

3 medium firm but ripe peaches (about 1 pound or 454g), peeled and sliced (about 2 cups sliced)

⅓ cup (100g) thinly sliced red onion (see Tip, below)

1 tablespoon good balsamic vinegar

Preheat a grill for medium direct heat (350°F–450°F, or 175°C–230°C).

Meanwhile, remove half the orange zest in fine shreds and the other half in long coils. Squeeze the orange juice into a small bowl. Set aside.

Brush each flatbread with the olive oil and sprinkle generously with salt and pepper. Repeat on the flip side. Grill the breads until they puff slightly and grill marks appear, about 3 to 4 minutes total, flipping once halfway through. Cool to room temperature.

Season the mascarpone with ⅛ teaspoon each salt and pepper, the shredded orange zest (save the coils), and 2 tablespoons of the orange juice. Stir until smooth. Divide among the flatbreads, spreading thickly. Top with the peach slices and red onion slices. Use a heavy knife to cut each flatbread into thirds (if oblong) or quarters (if round).

Place the vinegar in a small microwave-safe bowl, and microwave on full power until slightly thickened and reduced by about half, about 1 minute. (Use caution when removing.) Drizzle over the flatbreads. Garnish with the coils of orange zest. Serve immediately.

Tip: If you have a mandoline, use it on its thinnest setting to slice the onion.

Persimmons

With rutabagas, cherimoyas, and kohlrabi in the world, who has time to figure out persimmons? Sure, if you've grown up eating them you can tell your Fuyus from your Hachiyas, but the rest of us are sure to wonder what's up with the weird looking tomatoes with the bright orange skin.

The Fuyu variety is firm, and it shines when sliced into salads. Squat and compact, with a leaflike cap, its thin skin gives way to perfumed, velvety flesh. This is the persimmon for the novice and the risk-averse. If it's hard, no matter—it's delicious. If it's soft, no matter—it's still delicious. Win-win.

Hachiyas are level two persimmons. They're for those who can wait patiently for the shiny fruit to mellow and ripen. Eat it too soon and it will suck your mouth dry like a vacuum cleaner. Happily, its astringency fades when the fruit decides it's ready, and not a moment sooner. Hachiya purée is prized in cakes, preserves, muffins, and English-style puddings.

Tip: Peeling persimmons is a matter of personal choice. I find that leaving a Fuyu's skin intact makes it easier to slice, plus I like the contrast in textures. Ripe Hachiyas are soft enough that you can cut them in half and spoon out their flesh, then purée or sieve it, if desired.

SIMPLE USES FOR PERSIMMONS:

salad = Mâche + Fuyus + sunflower seeds + cucumber

tea bread = Hachiya purée + flour + baking soda + brown sugar + milk + butter + eggs + dates + pecans

lettuce cups = slivered Fuyus + jicama + mint + cilantro + basil + butter lettuce

Persimmon Apple Radicchio Stacks

Entertaining the queen, your boss, or your future in-laws?
Here's a sophisticated stacked salad that takes just minutes to compose.
Keeping the peels on helps create the neatest slices.

SERVES 4

¼ cup (60ml) extra-virgin olive oil

2 tablespoons apple cider vinegar

Coarse salt and coarse
  ground pepper

2 medium ripe but firm Fuyu
  persimmons

1 large or 2 medium Granny Smith
  apples, unpeeled

1 small head radicchio
  (you'll use about 10 to 12 leaves)

In a large bowl, whisk the oil and vinegar. Season generously with salt and pepper.

Using a mandoline set to medium thickness (or your best knife skills), slice the persimmon from the bottom up, horizontally. (Discard the leafy top.) Add the slices to the vinaigrette, turn to coat, then remove with a slotted spoon to a large plate. Now slice the apple, also medium thick, plucking out the seeds after slicing. (This produces a prettier result than coring the fruit first.) Add to the vinaigrette, then remove and pile next to the persimmons. Remove 10 to 12 leaves of radicchio and tear into large pieces. Coat with dressing, then pile on the plate.

To assemble the stacks, lay 1 persimmon slice on the bottom of a serving plate. Top with an apple slice and a piece of radicchio. Repeat until you have 3 to 4 layers. Sprinkle with coarse salt and pepper. Compose the remaining stacks. Serve.

Sugar Pie Pumpkins

Save massive pumpkins for carving and your stoop, and buy petite sugar pies for cooking and baking instead. Two- to four-pound pie pumpkins make a nice alternative to canned pumpkin purée, plus you can play catch with them if you're bored.

To use, hack fresh pumpkins into wedges, or peel (good luck) and dice them up for soups, stews, or risottos. Caramelizing the pieces in the oven gives them a sweet flavor and a savage tan.

Let's make a deal: you roast a fresh pumpkin once, just to compare the results with what you're used to from a can. If you're not suitably impressed with the outcome, revert to the tins and I shall never mention this conversation again.

Tip: To roast a 2- to $2\frac{1}{2}$-pound (about 1kg) sugar pie pumpkin for homemade purée, preheat the oven to 400°F (200°C) with the rack in the center position. Line a rimmed baking sheet with foil and slick with oil. Carve out the stem, halve the pumpkin vertically, and scrape out the seeds and strings. Roast cut-side down until the skin puckers and browns and the flesh is very tender, 55 to 60 minutes. Cool, peel, and purée in a food processor until completely smooth. Scrape into a cheesecloth-lined strainer set over a large bowl. Cover loosely and refrigerate overnight to drain. Yield: About 2 cups (500ml) purée

SIMPLE USES FOR SUGAR PIE PUMPKINS:

pot de crème = pumpkin purée + yolks + cream + sugar + vanilla + cinnamon + ginger + clove + nutmeg

roasted pumpkin with minted yogurt = peeled sugar pie pumpkin wedges + oil + sugar + yogurt + mint + garlic + coriander

soup = roasted pumpkin cubes + lentils + stock + olive oil + carrots + onions + garlic + cumin + lemon

Roasted Pumpkin Gingerbread

My funny and talented friend Jill O'Connor, author of five cookbooks, including
Sticky, Chewy, Messy, Gooey *and* Sticky, Chewy, Messy, Gooey Treats for Kids, *generously
shared her wonderful pumpkin cake recipe with me. Because I've opted to use freshly roasted
pumpkin (for tips on roasting fresh pumpkin, see page 109), please start the cake one day
ahead to give the purée ample time to drain. Alternatively, substitute pure canned pumpkin.*

···················· **MAKES ONE 10-INCH BUNDT CAKE** ····················

2³/₄ cups (344g) all-purpose flour

2 teaspoons baking soda

½ teaspoon baking powder

½ teaspoon kosher salt

1 tablespoon ground ginger

2 teaspoons ground cinnamon

½ teaspoon ground nutmeg

½ teaspoon ground cardamom

¼ teaspoon ground cloves

¼ teaspoon ground white pepper

½ cup (118ml) canola oil

½ cup (118ml) molasses

½ cup (170g) honey

¹/₃ cup (67g) packed dark muscovado or brown sugar

1½ cups (680g) freshly roasted (or canned) pumpkin purée

1 cup (237ml) low-fat buttermilk

3 eggs

Preheat the oven to 350°F (175°C). Set the rack in the center position.

Coat a 10-inch (25.5cm) Bundt pan generously with nonstick cooking spray. If the pan is fluted, leave it sprayed but unlined. If it's straight, line the bottom with parchment and spray the parchment. In a large bowl, sift the flour, baking soda, baking powder, salt, and all the spices.

In a large saucepan, combine the oil, molasses (unsulphured is best), honey, and brown sugar. Stir over medium heat until the sugar melts. Cool slightly. Whisk in the pumpkin purée, buttermilk, and eggs, one at a time. Whisk in the flour mixture in three additions.

Pour the batter into the prepared pan. Bake for 45 to 50 minutes, or until a skewer inserted near the center comes out clean.

Cool the cake in the pan on a wire rack for 20 minutes. Unmold and finish cooling completely to room temperature. Slice and serve. (Store any leftover cake in the refrigerator. Bring to room temperature before serving.)

Yams

Poor yams. Everyone thinks they're sweet potatoes.

Poor sweet potatoes. Everyone thinks they're yams.

Look, they're different species, but the use of these two terms has been muddled for so long that it would take a person far more powerful than I to change the popular lexicon, at least in the United States where confusing these two is something of a birthright.

I'm partial to jewel yams, those ruddy-looking tubers that can be slim and uniform or wildly curvaceous. Slice one open and its insides glow. In a pinch, they could serve as a beacon for sailors at sea.

Bake yams until soft, slit their tops, and push out their flesh before crowning it with butter. Or mash the very life out of them, sprinkling in brown sugar, cardamom, raw eggs and cinnamon, then bake them again until smooth and custardy.

Of course, one can only get away with that much richness so often. On a standard weeknight I'm much more apt to roast them in wedges, rubbing them down with oil and spices like they're lolling about at a spa.

Tip: When buying jewel yams for mashing, an irregular shape makes no difference. But if planning to bake them whole or roast them in wedges, choose jewel yams of uniform thickness.

SIMPLE USES FOR YAMS:

curry = yams + oil + onion + ginger + garlic + curry + cauliflower + chickpeas + water + canned tomatoes

side = mashed yams + lime + green onions

tian = thin-sliced yams + thin-sliced Yukon gold potatoes + zucchini + olive oil + garlic + thyme

Spiced Caramelized Yam Wedges

These yams develop an almost chewy crust from an hour long stay in the oven. Don't pull them out earlier.

$^3/_4$ teaspoon kosher salt

$^1/_4$ teaspoon freshly ground black pepper

$^1/_4$ teaspoon ancho chile powder

$^1/_8$ teaspoon cayenne pepper (for a subtle heat), or slightly more, to taste

1 teaspoon dark brown sugar

2 medium yams (1 pound, or 454g, each), peeled and sliced into 1/2-inch-thick (1.25cm) half-circles

1 tablespoon olive oil

Preheat the oven to 400°F (200°C). In a small bowl, mix the salt, black pepper, chile powder, cayenne, and brown sugar.

Mound the yams on a rimmed baking sheet. Add the oil and spice mix. Mix thoroughly, making sure to coat every piece. Spread into a single layer with room between each piece.

Roast in the center of the oven for 1 hour, turning the pieces halfway through, until a dark crust forms on both sides, Let stand 5 minutes before serving.

Tip: For best results, do not line your sheet pan, and choose yams that are an even thickness from end to end.

YELLOW

Bananas

Leon loved bananas. I mean, my maternal grandfather Leon must have loved bananas for he ate them every day that I knew him. This trait wound its way down the family tree to my younger son's branch, a branch so banana laden I fear it may someday snap and drop him to the ground.

Bananas are easy. Yes, they have potassium and, yes, they come in bright yellow casings, but really, the reasons to keep bananas on hand are straightforward. One, they rot, which creates a moral imperative to bake banana bread with great regularity. Two, they can be frozen, which creates a moral imperative to whip up frequent smoothies. And three—and people forget this, so please pay attention—they taste unbelievable when cooked, which creates a moral imperative to fry up gooey banana fritters or flambé boozy Bananas Foster or grill chocolaty banana boats while camping with your Girl Scout troop. If you've never done these things, please go directly to jail, do not pass go, and do not collect your $200.

Tip: Throwing bananas away is never justified. As soon as yours are past prime, freeze slices on a plate until hard, then transfer to a zip-top freezer bag for several months. Pop into shakes, smoothies, or your mouth.

SIMPLE USES FOR BANANAS:

shake = frozen bananas + Medjool dates + flaxseed + milk
fritters = bananas + flour + sugar + baking powder + salt + milk + eggs + canola oil
sandwich = bananas + peanut butter + honey + whole-wheat bread

Chocolate-Flecked Banana Buttermilk Pancakes

These are a serious weekend favorite in my banana-loving house. After you flip the pancakes, the heat from the griddle caramelizes and browns the bananas, delivering an oozy sweetness you can't get from any other fruit. The batter keeps well in a covered glass jar in the fridge, so if you've got some left over, enjoy bonus pancake breakfasts during the week.

MAKES 30 TO 35 PANCAKES

3 cups (375g) all-purpose flour

1 tablespoon baking powder

$\frac{1}{2}$ teaspoon baking soda

$\frac{1}{4}$ teaspoon kosher salt

2 teaspoons sugar

Zest of 1 lemon

4 tablespoons butter, melted and slightly cooled

$2\frac{2}{3}$ cups (631ml) buttermilk

4 eggs

$\frac{1}{2}$ cup (113g) mini chocolate chips

4 bananas, thinly sliced

Maple syrup, for serving

In a food processor, whiz all the ingredients except the chocolate chips and bananas for 30 seconds. Turn off the machine, scrape the sides to incorporate any clingy flour bits, then process again for 30 seconds longer. Transfer to a large bowl. Stir in the chocolate chips.

Heat a cast-iron griddle over medium-high heat until a drop of water sizzles and evaporates. Coat with nonstick spray or butter. Portion out the batter using a standard ice cream scoop or small cup measure. Lay 3 banana slices atop each pancake. Cook until the undersides are golden brown, about $1\frac{1}{2}$ minutes, then flip and cook the other side until the bananas have caramelized and browned, about 1 minute longer.

Serve with maple syrup.

Corn

He's the loudest vendor at the farmers' market. I don't know his name, but every summer without fail he booms for hours on end: "Brentwood corn! Sweeter than my mother-in-law! If it's not the best corn you've ever had, bring the cobs back for a refund!"

The first time I heard his schtick, I laughed. Clever! Original! I love mother-in-law jokes! And then I realized that with any luck, one day I too will be a mother-in-law, and I'll want more respect.

Now while the thought of my children getting married makes me happy in theory, if they become corn farmers and their marketing strategy is to honor me by bellowing, "Fresh corn! Not as sweet as my mother-in-law!" I'd be super flattered, but they wouldn't sell too much corn.

This makes me anxious, so I wander towards the zucchini.

Tip: When cutting corn from the cob, give yourself wide berth and use your largest cutting board. Better yet, set a board inside a rimmed baking sheet so the kernels can't run rampant.

SIMPLE USES FOR CORN:

quesadillas = whole-wheat tortillas + roasted corn + pepper Jack cheese + red pepper + salsa
salad = corn + black beans + cotija cheese + shredded romaine + chile vinaigrette
corn pudding = corn + diced onion + diced bell peppers + cream + eggs + Cheddar cheese

Corn with Cilantro-Lime Salt

Fresh, bright, and summery, this simple side perks up sweet corn with classic Mexican flavors. Be sure your cilantro leaves are completely dry before mincing them with the lime and salt. You don't want them to clump up.

··· **SERVES 4** ···

4 ears corn, husks and silks stripped and discarded

³⁄₄ cup (28g) loosely packed cilantro leaves (no stems), rinsed and pat completely dry

1 lime

¹⁄₂ teaspoon kosher salt

1 tablespoon unsalted butter, melted

Bring a large pot of water to boil. Boil the corn until tender, 3 to 5 minutes, depending on its freshness. Drain.

Mound the cilantro leaves on a cutting board. Zest the lime so that fine shreds fall directly on the cilantro. Sprinkle the salt on top. Using a heavy knife, mince the cilantro, zest, and salt together. Scrape into a small bowl.

When the corn is cool enough to handle, cut the kernels from the cobs using a downward motion. Transfer to a serving bowl.

Drizzle the butter over the corn. Sprinkle with the cilantro-lime salt, and squeeze with lime juice to taste. Toss to coat. Serve immediately.

Tip: When fresh corn is not in season, substitute 3 cups (850g) of frozen, cooked corn.

Lemons

After we moved to California, I wanted one thing only: a lemon-flavored piece of the agricultural pie. This would mean an all-access pass to sunny curds, tangy mousses, bright sauces, and crisp lemonade from my yard's own all-you-can-drink canteen.

So we got a dwarf lemon tree.

I look at that lemon tree every day when I flow in and out the front door. I see everything in it: hope, productivity, magic, wonder, sweetness, and light. I see the passage of time. My children have grown with that tree year in and year out.

Today, they're taller than its branches. They must bend to twist a fruit off its limbs. That tree's our family pet and if we ever move, it's coming with.

Tip: I'm partial to Meyer lemons, which have less bite than the Eureka and Lisbon varieties. If substituting one type for another, always adjust the amount to your liking.

SIMPLE USES FOR LEMONS:

risotto = butter + shallots + Arborio rice + white wine + stock + lemon zest + juice + pecorino

avgolemono (Greek lemon soup) = stock + rice + egg yolks + lemon juice + parsley

curd = eggs yolks + sugar + lemon juice + zest + butter

Agave Meyer Lemonade

I can think of no better way to honor the
bright, uplifting flavor of sunny lemons than
with this fresh, agave-sweetened lemonade.

MAKES 1^1/$_4$ QUARTS, OR ROUGHLY
SIX 7-OUNCE SERVINGS

8 medium Meyer lemons
^{1}/$_2$ to ^{2}/$_3$ cup (170-340g) agave nectar, or to taste

4 cups (0.95l) cold water, preferably refrigerated
Ice

Squeeze enough lemons (6 to 7) into a 2-cup (500ml) glass measure to yield 1^1/$_4$ cups (300ml) of juice. Strain into a large pitcher. Whisk in the agave nectar, beginning with ^{1}/$_2$ cup (118ml) and adding more to taste. Pour in the water. Whisk to combine.

   Chill, covered, until ready to serve.

   Distribute the lemonade among ice-filled glasses. Slice the remaining lemon (you may even have one left over), and float 1 slice in each glass. Serve immediately.

Pineapples

Fifteen years ago, I married a Texan. My husband's extended family recently gathered at a fishing lodge in East Texas, a spot the family had gone to for years. Though I'm not much of an angler, I happily came along.

We spent long days fishing, chasing fireflies, and filling our bellies with deep-fried country fare. Hush puppies, biscuits, and plenty of pie. And that was just breakfast.

Towards the end of the weekend, my husband's cousin unearthed a pineapple and passed out chunks as we lazed about on the porch. I welcomed its bright acidity, a contrast to the heavier food we'd been inhaling.

When I returned home, I bought a pineapple, too, and skewered spears up for the grill.

I loved its simplicity, but I did miss all that pie.

Tip: To prep a pineapple, slice the bottom flat and lop off its thorny crown. Then quarter the pineapple lengthwise, set the quarters on their sides, slice out the cores, and slide off the "meat" off with your knife. I find this easier than peeling the pineapple and gouging out its eyes.

SIMPLE USES FOR PINEAPPLES:

salad = pineapple + black beans + grape tomatoes + avocado + chile-honey vinaigrette
entrée & salsa = vegetable quesadillas + pineapple + serrano chiles + cilantro + lime
Latin batido = pineapple + ice + milk + honey + rum

Grilled Five-Spice Pineapple Kabobs

Grilling fruit concentrates its flavors. Here, pineapple chunks are brushed with oil and spices and then tossed on the grill. Go savory, serving with Red Curry Glazed Butternut Squash (page 76), or sweet, atop coconut ice cream (page 279).

·· **MAKES 6 SERVINGS** ··

1 pineapple (preferably "Gold"), peeled, cored, and cut lengthwise into sixths

6 skewers (if wooden, presoak for 30 minutes)

2 tablespoons canola oil

1½ teaspoons Chinese five-spice powder

Cracked black pepper, optional

Preheat a clean grill or grill pan over medium-high heat.

Cut each pineapple spear into 6 chunks. Thread 6 chunks flat onto each skewer, leaving some space between each piece. Set on a baking sheet.

Brush all sides with canola oil and sprinkle with five-spice powder. Rub any oil or spices that fell onto the baking sheet back onto the fruit.

Grill until dark grill marks appear, turning two or three times, about 8 minutes total.

Pomelos

If you crossed a volleyball with a grapefruit, you'd get a pomelo.
Alternately spelled pommelo or pummelo, this large, Southeast Asian citrus will surprise you with its low acidity and friendly, approachable sweetness. Its juicy flesh is best enjoyed when segments are released completely from their thick, clingy membranes, so take your time excising. Grab two knives: a large one to slice away the squishy body armor, and a smaller one to extract the sweet fruit and shave away its pith.

Pomelos are easy to love straight up, or in refreshing salads, which is how they're enjoyed throughout Asia. Count on two eaters for each pomelo. If you don't have a best friend, a child, a spouse, or a neighbor, now's a good time to find one.

Tip: When choosing pomelos, aim for heft rather than girth. Larger specimens may simply harbor more sofa-cushiony internal padding, which is fine if you need an extra pillow but less useful if you want a snack.

SIMPLE USES FOR POMELOS:

candied peel = pomelo rind + sugar + water
breakfast = pomelo + pomegranate seeds + honey + lime
salad = pomelo + bean sprouts + Thai basil + mint + chile + peanuts

Maple Pomelo Parfaits with Streamlined Granola

This light fruit, yogurt, and granola parfait makes a pretty counterpart to heavier breakfast and brunch fare. Just be sure to give yourself time to excavate the pomelo flesh from its peel. Happily, you'll have gobs of granola left over—a boon since it stores quite well for days.

**SERVES 4, WITH EXCESS GRANOLA
(MAKES 4½ CUPS OR 675g GRANOLA)**

¼ cup (60ml) vegetable oil

¼ cup (85g) honey

½ teaspoon vanilla extract

2 cups (180g) old-fashioned
  rolled oats

1½ cups (120g) unsweetened,
  desiccated coconut

1 cup (142g) whole almonds
  (or nut of your choice), chopped

¼ teaspoon kosher salt

2 medium or 1 large pomelo
  (about 3½ pounds, or 1.6kg)

1 cup (237ml) nonfat Greek yogurt

1 to 2 tablespoons pure maple
  syrup, plus more for drizzling

To make the granola: Preheat the oven to 325°F (165°C) with the rack in the center position. Line a rimmed baking sheet with parchment. In a large bowl, whisk the oil, honey, and vanilla until smooth. Stir in the oats, coconut, nuts, and salt and turn to coat everything evenly. Spread on the prepared baking sheet. Bake for 25 to 30 minutes, stirring every 8 minutes, until golden brown.

Meanwhile, prep the pomelos. Set the fruit on a large cutting board with the stems ends sideways. Slice off the ends to expose the flesh. Turn the fruit onto a flat end, and, using your knife at an angle, curve down the sides, exposing as much juicy flesh as possible. Continue until you've peeled the entire fruit. (Clean off any stubborn pith with a paring knife.) Slice each section free of its membrane and place in a small bowl. Squeeze the membrane into a cup and add any juice on the cutting board. You'll have a scant ½ cup (118ml) of juice.

In a small bowl, stir the yogurt and 1 to 2 tablespoons of both the maple syrup and the pomelo juice, to taste.

Divide the pomelo, granola, and yogurt among four 6- to 8-ounce (178- to 237ml) glasses, making 2 layers. Finish with a drizzle of maple syrup, if desired. (Leftover granola may be stored for several days in an airtight container.)

Squash Blossoms

❧

Most people give flowers. Some people eat them.

When we first started dating, my husband, Colin, ate a rose petal to profess his love for me. His face told the truth: this was a phenomenally bad idea.

Tastier (and safer) edible flowers abound, from hibiscus to calendula to borage. Perhaps none is more popular than the sun-drenched squash or zucchini blossom, a glorious yellow bloom often stuffed with cheese and fried until crisp. You can certainly buy the flowers, but they're pricy. Instead, just pluck them from your garden, assuming you haven't sprayed.

If you don't grow them yourself, find a friend who does. Plenty of people grow zucchini, and most don't give the flowers a second thought.

Tip: Be sure to open each blossom carefully and rinse it thoroughly to flush out any tiny bugs that may call your blossom home.

SIMPLE USES FOR SQUASH BLOSSOMS:

cheese-stuffed fried squash blossoms = squash blossoms + ricotta + Parmesan + fines herbes + egg + flour + soda water + oil

golden omelet = squash blossoms + eggs + turmeric + yellow summer squash + goat cheese

squash blossom Caprese = squash blossoms + tomato + mozzarella + basil

Beer-Battered Squash Blossoms

This crispy snack goes great with cold beer, so buy a few extra bottles while you're out.

½ cup (62.5g) all-purpose flour

¼ cup (55g) cornstarch

½ teaspoon turmeric

1 (12-ounce, or 355ml) bottle of beer (you'll use half; drink the rest)

Kosher salt

Canola oil

10 to 12 medium squash blossoms, cleaned and pat dry, stems and stamens removed

Line a large plate with paper towels. Fit a deep-fry or candy thermometer in a deep saucepot. Pour canola oil to a depth of ½ inch (1.25cm) in the pot and heat over medium high until it reaches 350°F.

In a medium bowl, whisk the flour, cornstarch, and turmeric to combine. Whisk in half the bottle of beer. Let stand while the oil gets hot.

Dip 2 or 3 blossoms in the batter to coat. Fry until golden and crisp, 60 to 90 seconds total, turning once. Remove with a slotted spoon to the paper towels. Season immediately with salt. Repeat with the remaining blossoms.

Checkout Receipt

Newton Branch
(804) 472-3820
Wed Oct 28 2015

****

Mark Bittman's Kitchen
Express : 404 in
*DUE: Wed Nov 11 2015

Ripe : a fresh, colorful
approach to fr
*DUE: Wed Nov 11 2015

TOTAL : 2

Visit us online at
LibraryPoint.org

Yellow Onions

The word *onion* is derived from the Latin word *unio*, meaning "single white pearl." That said, I wouldn't string them on a necklace.

Staples of pantries, root cellars, and soup pots worldwide, onions are true workhorses. You can batter and deep-fry them, caramelize them, roast them, grill them, or mince them raw. You can pair them with garlic and ginger to jump-start any stir-fry, dump them in a slow cooker with butter until they mellow, encrust them with cheese in a soup or quiche, or toss them atop a piping hot pizza.

For those accustomed to relegating yellow onions to the supporting actor category, I challenge you to bring them front and center. Onions are people, too, and they deserve a turn in the limelight.

Tip: Theories abound for how to slice raw onions without sobbing, including wearing goggles, burning candles, and working under a stovetop vent. Do what works for you, and wear contact lenses, if you have them.

SIMPLE USES FOR YELLOW ONIONS:

French onion soup = olive oil + sliced onions + water + parsley stems + bay leaf + thyme + French bread + Gruyère

Israeli salad = tomatoes + cucumbers + diced sweet onions + lemon vinaigrette + parsley + mint

grilled onions and peppers = sliced yellow onions + mixed bell peppers + olive oil + salt + vinegar

Caramelized Onion Asiago Tart

This pretty lunch tart or first course requires no special skill but does require a bit of patience. Patience to wait for the frozen puff pastry to thaw, patience to wait for the onions to properly soften, and patience—above all—to wait for the tart to cool so you don't scorch the roof of your mouth.

················· MAKES 6 LARGE OR 12 PETITE COCKTAIL-SIZED PORTIONS ·················

2 tablespoons extra-virgin olive oil

4 medium yellow onions (about 2 pounds, or 907g), peeled, halved, and sliced

Kosher salt and freshly ground black pepper

1 teaspoon brown sugar

$\frac{1}{2}$ teaspoon white wine vinegar (or plain distilled white vinegar)

1 sheet frozen puff pastry (from a 17.3 oz, or 490g, package), thawed according to package directions

1 egg, lightly beaten

$\frac{2}{3}$ cup (36g) oil-packed sun-dried tomatoes (18 to 20)

$\frac{1}{2}$ cup (40g) shredded Asiago cheese (substitute Parmesan, if desired)

Preheat the oven to 400°F (200°C). Line a baking sheet with parchment.

Place your largest skillet over medium-high heat. Add the olive oil, onions, $1\frac{1}{2}$ teaspoons salt, and $\frac{1}{2}$ teaspoon pepper. Sauté, stirring frequently, until the onions are translucent, about 10 minutes. (Raise the heat, if necessary, to get the onions going, but make sure they do not burn.) Add the brown sugar and vinegar, reduce the heat to medium, and continue cooking until the onions are sweet and soft, 15 to 20 minutes longer. Remove from the heat and let cool slightly.

Meanwhile, prepare the pastry. On a floured board and using a floured rolling pin, roll out the thawed pastry into a 12 x 10-inch (24.5 x 30.5cm) rectangle. Transfer to the lined baking sheet. Refrigerate until needed.

When the onions have cooled, remove the pastry from the refrigerator and brush the entire surface with the egg. Reserve 6 whole sun-dried tomatoes, then mince the rest and spread thinly over the egg, leaving a $\frac{1}{2}$-inch (1.25cm) border. Sprinkle the cheese over the tomatoes and the onions, thickly, over the cheese.

Bake in the center of the oven for 15 minutes. Remove the tart from the oven, briefly, in order to lay the remaining whole sun-dried tomatoes on top, marking 6 portions (think 2 horizontal rows of 3). Continue baking until the pastry is puffed and golden brown, about 10 minutes longer. Slice and serve.

GREEN

Green Apples

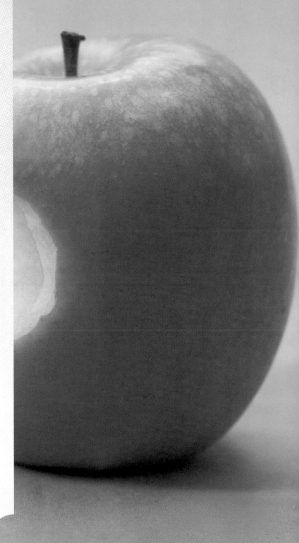

In the nineteenth century, Mr. and Mrs. Smith had children, moved to Australia, and bought a farm. One day, apparently, Mrs. Smith discovered some crab apple seedlings on the farm had mutated, becoming what are known, in her honor, as Granny Smiths.

Sadly, Mrs. Smith died before she could see the impact of her discovery. I for one would like to offer her posthumous thanks, along with a standing ovation.

With a pleasant, sour bite, Granny Smiths pair well with creamy or cheesy dishes, cutting any richness with a tingling lift. Try the Gruyère-Crusted Leeks and Apples (page 206) as evidence.

But green apples are welcome in sweet recipes, too, like my twist on charoset that follows and in your favorite apple pie. Never underestimate the impact of a granny.

Tip: Granny Smiths are equally good both raw and cooked.

SIMPLE USES FOR GRANNY SMITH APPLES:

panini = grilled Swiss cheese + apples + pumpernickel

pommes caramelle or French baked apples with caramel sauce = apples + light corn syrup + brown sugar + vanilla + cream + Calvados

salad = apples + Roquefort + Dijon vinaigrette

Green Apple Charoset

Charoset, a mixture of apples, nuts, and sweet wine that symbolizes the mortar Jewish slaves used when laying bricks in Egypt, has always been my favorite part of the Passover meal. This pale green version is a modern twist.

MAKES 5 CUPS

3 large Granny Smith apples, unpeeled, cored, finely diced (about $4\frac{1}{4}$ cups)

$1\frac{1}{2}$ cups (140g) toasted pecans, finely chopped

$1\frac{1}{2}$ teaspoons granulated sugar

$\frac{1}{2}$ teaspoon ground cinnamon

$\frac{1}{4}$ cup (60ml) sweet white wine, such as Riesling

Combine all the ingredients in a medium serving bowl. Serve immediately, or cover and refrigerate for several hours. (It might brown, but it's supposed to look like mortar anyway, so don't sweat it.)

Tip: To toast pecans, place in a single layer in a preheated 350°F (175°C) oven for about 8 minutes, shaking the pan every now and again.

Artichokes

Poor artichokes. So misunderstood. With thorns screaming "Step back, Mister" and tender hearts inviting affection, these crazy vegetables—sorry, *thistles*—alternately confuse and seduce. No wonder people are afraid of them.

Fact is, artichokes are not difficult to cook, but they do need to be prepped slowly and deliberately, and you must take care not to impale your tender fingers while handling them. For larger artichokes, snip off the thorns with scissors, peel the stem until it's pale, and pare off leaves around the base. Then quarter the artichokes with a heavy knife, and scrape out the hairy choke (world's worst phrase), adding the cleaned quarters to lemony water as you go. Put on some tunes; time will fly! Boil the quarters until tender and the leaves ease out with little resistance. You can also boil artichokes whole, but then you'll need to deal with the choke after the fact, and the only thing worse than a hairy choke is a hot hairy choke, if you know what I mean.

Of course, you can always opt for choke-free baby artichokes instead. That's what I've done in the following recipe. Well, that, and plied them with wine.

Tip: Look for bright green, unblemished artichokes with tightly bundled leaves. Store in the refrigerator.

SIMPLE USES FOR ARTICHOKES:

Italian-style = artichokes + lemon + garlic + breadcrumbs + butter
starter = artichokes + capers + homemade aïoli
salad = marinated artichokes + hearts of palm + chickpeas + fresh herbs

Wine-Braised Artichokes with Feta and Orecchiette

The flavorful braising liquid in this sophisticated pasta dish reduces into a lovely sauce, which both coats the artichokes and slides into the crevices of the pasta. Toasted pine nuts, if you have some, would make a nice addition.

························· **SERVES 4 TO 6** ·························

Kosher salt

8 ounces (227g) orecchiette or medium pasta shells

Juice of ½ lemon

1½ pounds (680g) baby artichokes (about 9)

3 tablespoons extra-virgin olive oil

3 garlic cloves, peeled and smashed

½ cup (118ml) vegetable stock

½ cup (118ml) dry white wine

2 ounces (57g) creamy Greek feta, crumbled

3 tablespoons drained capers

½ cup (28g) chopped fresh parsley

Pepper

Cook the pasta in salted water according to package directions, reserving 1 cup (237ml) of the pasta cooking water.

Meanwhile, squeeze the lemon juice into a large bowl of cold water. To trim the artichokes, pull off and discard the hard outermost leaves. Eventually you will come to a point where the leaves are tender and soft, half green and half yellow. Use a sharp, heavy knife to cut off the top (green) portion. Slice the stem level with the base. Quarter each artichoke lengthwise, then toss in the lemon bath. Repeat with the remaining artichokes.

Place the oil and garlic in a large skillet over medium-low heat for about 3 minutes, so the garlic can slowly warm. Using a slotted spoon, transfer the artichokes to a double thickness of paper towels and pat dry, then carefully add to the skillet. Raise the heat to medium high, and sauté for about 5 minutes.

Add the stock and wine to the skillet and bring to a boil. Reduce the heat, cover, and cook until the artichokes are tender, about 10 minutes. Uncover, raise the heat again, and simmer for an additional 3 minutes so the liquid reduces slightly. Transfer the drained pasta to the skillet, along with the feta, capers, and parsley. Spoon in a few tablespoons of the reserved cooking liquid to loosen the sauce, if desired. Heat through, season with pepper, and serve immediately.

Asparagus

I would like to fill the world's pencil boxes with asparagus. Just once, just for fun. Imagine if schoolchildren everywhere discovered long, slender spears in their backpacks instead of boring number two pencils. Who wouldn't be tickled to find asparagus nestled quietly among the protractors, compasses, and liquid paper? Math class would be much more interesting.

Kids would stick the asparagus behind their ears, tap them like drumsticks, or pen secret messages to each other in invisible asparagus ink.

Later, at cheerleading practice after school, twirlers would toss their asparagus high in the air, *up, up, up!*, then catch them with a dramatic, crowd-pleasing flourish.

Or, I suppose, we could just eat the asparagus. That would be fine, too.

Tip: Ice cold asparagus spears make an excellent crudité. Boil until just barely al dente and immediately shock in a bowl of ice water. Pat dry and refrigerate, wrapped lightly in paper towels, until ready to serve (preferably with a creamy dip).

SIMPLE USES FOR ASPARAGUS:

risotto = onion + Arborio rice + butter + stock + white wine + Parmesan + asparagus + lemon
soup = leeks + asparagus + garlic + stock + cream
tart = asparagus + morel mushrooms + savory custard + puff pastry + Comté cheese

Grilled Asparagus with Chopped Egg and Champagne Vinaigrette

This light lunch offers classic French flavors with little effort, and it's my favorite way to eat asparagus. If you scale up the recipe, count on one egg for every two diners.

· SERVES 2 FOR LUNCH ·

1 large egg

1 teaspoon Dijon mustard

1 tablespoon champagne vinegar

3 tablespoons olive oil, divided

Kosher salt and freshly ground
  black pepper

1 pound (454g) medium asparagus,
  woody ends snapped off

Leaves from 1 sprig fresh tarragon

Preheat a grill to medium heat (350°F to 450°F or 175°C to 230°C). Scrape the grates clean.

While the grill preheats, cook the egg. Place 1 egg in a small saucepan and cover with cold water. Bring to a boil. Remove from the heat, cover, and let stand for exactly 12 minutes. Plunge into cold water, peel, and finely chop.

In a small bowl, whisk the mustard, vinegar, and 2 tablespoons of the olive oil. Season with salt and pepper.

Place the asparagus on a rimmed baking sheet and drizzle with the remaining olive oil. Sprinkle with salt and pepper, rubbing the oil and seasonings in with clean fingers. Transfer the asparagus to the hot grill, setting the spears perpendicular to the grates. Cook, covered, until evenly blistered and slightly charred, turning with tongs once or twice during cooking, about 4 minutes total. Return to the baking sheet.

Drizzle the asparagus with half the vinaigrette. Transfer to a serving platter. Sprinkle with the chopped egg and tarragon. Serve, passing the remaining dressing alongside.

Avocados

Silken, creamy, sexy. Avocados, so rich in heart-happy fat, kept my family together back in 2004.

I'd been living quite happily in the Boston suburbs. Life was filled with friends, kids, my dog, my friends' kids, my friends' dogs, my dog's friends, and then—boom. My husband got a job offer out in California. I should have been happy, but who wants to change coats, much less coasts? I was miserable.

Then, moving day came. On the January day we left Boston, it was seven degrees. When our plane touched down in San Jose, it was seventy. That might have done it, but the thing that really sealed the deal, that proved I'd survive living out west, was the abundance of perfect avocados. I purchased some a few days later, their skin unblemished, their flesh smooth, their flavor sweet and mellow.

"Okay," I announced to no one. "I'll stay."

Tip: Seek firm avocados with no soft spots. Eat when they just barely give when pressed.

SIMPLE USES FOR AVOCADOS:

raw = unpeeled avocado half + olive oil in the cavity + lime juice + coarse salt
  (eat with a spoon)

layered salad = avocado + yellow tomato + buffalo mozzarella + pesto + toasted pine nuts

cold soup = avocado + yogurt + buttermilk + cucumber + garlic + herbs + chile + lime

Avocado Tangerine Salsa

Is it a salsa or a guacamole? Questions like this give me a headache.
Here's what's important: it's a vivid amalgamation of the two, with bright citrusy flavors
and a swift chile kick. The proportions are completely flexible and may be modified to suit your
taste. You can also swap blood oranges, Cara Cara oranges, or even navel oranges for
the tangerines. But no tomatoes! Double, triple, or sextuple the recipe to feed a crowd.

······································· **MAKES ABOUT 2 CUPS** ·······································

4 small seedless tangerines, peeled
and white pith removed

1 avocado, diced

¼ cup (40g) diced red onion

1 tablespoon minced fresh cilantro

1½ teaspoons minced jalapeño or
red chile, or to taste

1 teaspoon lime juice

Sea salt

Tortilla chips, for serving

Dice the peeled tangerines. Gently stir the avocado, onion, tangerines, cilantro, chile, and lime juice in a small bowl. Season with sea salt to taste. Serve with tortilla chips.

Bok Choy

If you've never cooked with bok choy, and you think your life has been fine, I'm here to tell you, as gently as I can, that it hasn't. It hasn't been fine at all. There has been something missing, and that thing is bok choy.

First, bok choy has a hilarious physical appearance. It looks like me on a rough morning.

Second, this popular Chinese staple—its *nom de plume* is actually Chinese white cabbage—makes every stir-fry better. It's economical, doesn't smell like cabbage, and offers a decisive, almost juicy crunch to everything from tofu to noodle bowls. Wherever you see sesame oil, ginger, garlic, scallions, or soy sauce, alone or in combination, in a bowl or on a plate, in a skillet or in a wok, that's a party begging for bok choy.

Tip: Bok choy comes in adult and baby varieties. If working with the latter, trim the bottoms, then halve or quarter them lengthwise before cooking. (Halves braise beautifully.) Full grown choy should be shredded crosswise with a knife, as in the following recipe for Miso Tofu Bok Choy. Refrigerate and use before the stalks yellow and the leaves wilt.

SIMPLE USES FOR BOK CHOY:

noodle bowl = bok choy + portobello mushrooms + soba noodles + toasted cashews + Sriracha

side = grilled baby bok choy + grilled red peppers + grilled red onions + soy sauce + sherry

braise = bok choy + vegetable stock + garlic + hoisin sauce

Miso Tofu Bok Choy

Bok choy can seem intimidating if you've never worked with it before, so just pretend it's a ter-rifically odd cabbage and shred it crosswise with your knife. Press the moisture from the tofu by wrap-ping it in several layers of paper towels and weighting it with a plate and a heavy can or jar. Change the paper towels once or twice as they get wet. Do this first, while you prep your remaining ingredients.

·· **SERVES 4 TO 6** ··

4 large garlic cloves, minced, divided

2 tablespoons red miso paste*

5 teaspoons (packed) grated fresh ginger

2 tablespoons rice vinegar

2 tablespoons sesame oil

1 tablespoon plus 1 teaspoon toasted peanut oil, divided

1 (14-ounce, or 397g) block firm tofu, pressed very dry (see head note), cut into ½-inch (1.25cm) dice

½ teaspoon cornstarch, plus more, if needed

1 head bok choy (about 2 pounds or 907g), shredded crosswise, rinsed well, and spun extremely dry

1 tablespoon black sesame seeds, for garnish

Add half the garlic to a mini food processor with the miso, ginger, vinegar, and sesame oil. Whiz until emulsified.

Set a large wok over high heat until drops of water sizzle and evaporate. Add 1 tablespoon of the peanut oil and the tofu, and stir-fry until the tofu begins to turn golden, about 5 minutes. Sprinkle in the cornstarch and con-tinue stir-frying until the tofu loses its sheen and gets one shade darker, 3 minutes longer. Transfer to a plate.

Add the remaining teaspoon of peanut oil and the remaining garlic to the wok. Stir-fry the garlic for 30 seconds, then add the bok choy. Toss until the greens wilt and the stalks are crisp-tender, about 2 minutes. Return the tofu to the wok, scrape in half the miso dressing, and heat through com-pletely. (If the dish looks watery, sprinkle in an additional 1 teaspoon corn-starch and continue cooking until the liquid evaporates.)

Garnish with the sesame seeds and pass the remaining miso dressing alongside. Serve immediately.

*Look for miso paste in Asian markets or natural food stores. You'll find the black sesame seeds there, too.

Tip: To make this a heartier and even more dramatic-looking dish, serve it over steamed black (sometimes labeled "forbidden") rice.

Broccoli

It was on a drive from San Jose down to San Diego, after Pacheco Pass but before the Grapevine, that I saw them: grove upon grove of broccoli trees. The landscape was riddled with them, huddled together, like teammates around a quarterback.

Were they really broccoli trees? Of course not, but with their stalky trunks and bushy heads and the brainwashing every child receives roundabout age three ("Eat your broccoli. Look how cute, just like little trees!"), they certainly gave that impression.

And I realized, with some measure of surprise and enlightenment, that when parents call broccoli little trees, this tactic is a sure-to-misfire abuse of parental power.

Look, we live in an age of environmental sensitivity. By the time they're in preschool, kids have already been taught the value of compost and the need to finger paint both sides of the page. Are they really going to eat little trees? No. They'll want to build nests in them for teeny birds with broken wings, and live in them when bulldozers come to chop them down, all the while blaring Joni Mitchell.

They paved paradise and put up a parking lot? Not on my watch, they didn't.

Tip: Purchase broccoli with tightly closed florets, keep refrigerated, and use before any signs of yellowing. Stalks are edible, too.

SIMPLE USES FOR BROCCOLI:

side = roasted broccoli + pearl barley + Dijon vinaigrette + capers

pesto = steamed broccoli + walnuts + olive oil + garlic + Parmesan

rice bowl = stir-fried broccoli (blanch first) + chile + soy sauce + cashew purée + tofu + rice

Broccoli Soup with Cheddar Croutons

A trio of Indian spices and a heap of cheesy croutons make this velvety, cream-free soup extra special. As with most soups, its flavor improves over time.

SERVES 6 TO 8

4 thick slices sturdy, bakery-style bread (pugliese, sourdough, country white, or the like)

1 teaspoon plus 2 tablespoons extra-virgin olive oil, divided

1½ cups (120g) grated Cheddar cheese, divided

1½ teaspoons cumin seeds

1 teaspoon ground coriander

½ teaspoon fennel seeds

Kosher salt and freshly ground black pepper

1 medium yellow onion, diced

2 pounds (907g) broccoli, stalks peeled and thinly sliced, florets finely chopped

2 cups (500ml) vegetable stock

¾ cup (178ml) water

½ cup (20g) packed chopped fresh Italian parsley

1 teaspoon fresh lemon juice

½ cup (110g) Greek yogurt (nonfat is fine)

Preheat the oven to 350°F (175°C). Line a rimmed baking sheet with parchment.

Dice the bread into ½-inch (1.25 cm) cubes. (You'll have about 4 cups or 600g). Toss on the prepared baking sheet with 1 teaspoon of the oil and 1 cup (80g) of the cheese. Spread in a single layer. (Most of the cheese will fall off the bread; carry on.) Bake for 20 minutes, until golden brown and bubbly, flipping the bread and lifting the melted cheese with a spatula twice during baking. Set aside.

Meanwhile, heat a large Dutch oven over medium-high heat. Add the remaining olive oil, the cumin seeds, coriander, fennel seeds, 1½ teaspoons salt, 1 teaspoon pepper, onion, and sliced broccoli stalks. Sauté until the vegetables are very tender, about 10 minutes, stirring frequently so the spices don't burn. Add the stock, water, and florets and bring to a boil. Reduce the heat and simmer, uncovered, for 15 minutes.

Remove from the heat and stir in the parsley. Purée using an immersion blender (you'll have to tilt the pot and work slowly) or a traditional blender, in batches. Stir in the lemon juice, yogurt, the remaining cheese, and additional salt, to taste. (The soup may be made ahead to this point, cooled, and refrigerated, covered, overnight.) Serve hot, thinning with a touch of water or stock, if desired, garnished with the Cheddar croutons.

Brussels Sprouts

At Refuel Restaurant & Bar in Vancouver, British Columbia, you can experience a Brussels sprouts revival. When I visited, the chef cooked them thrice: he blanched them, then flash sautéed them, then popped them in a hot oven. What emerged were crispy, deeply browned little cabbages slicked with butter that I inhaled like popcorn. Had I been given the option to supersize, I can assure you that I would have.

Here in California, the bulbous sprouts are often sold still attached to their stalks. These long, knobby branches resemble medieval torture apparatuses, which, I suppose if you're not a Brussels sprouts fan, might seem appropriate. Since I love them, though, I get a kick out of buying them this way whenever I can.

Plus, if anyone tries to snatch my purse as I head to my car, I can defend myself in a most unique manner.

Tip: Tiny Brussels sprouts, where available, are especially cute and cook quickly. Larger specimens should definitely be halved or quartered. Please do not boil full-size Brussels sprouts whole. No good can possibly come of that.

SIMPLE USES FOR BRUSSELS SPROUTS:

salad = raw, shaved Brussels sprouts + mustard-cider vinaigrette
side = mashed potatoes + crispy Brussels sprouts leaves
gratin = steamed, quartered Brussels sprouts + lemon + brown butter breadcrumbs

Fried Sage and Chestnut Brussels Sprouts

Rich chestnuts, crispy sage, and sweet currants add spark and complexity to these humble little cabbages. This holiday-friendly side comes together in fifteen minutes.

.... **SERVES 6** ....

3 tablespoons dried currants

3 tablespoons extra-virgin olive oil, divided

15 fresh sage leaves, stemmed

Kosher salt and freshly ground black pepper

1 pound (454g) small Brussels sprouts, halved

½ cup (about 3 ounces, or 85g) peeled and cooked chestnuts, chopped

Place the currants in a small bowl. Add boiling water just to cover. Set aside.

Heat a large, heavy skillet over medium-high heat for about 2 minutes. Add half the oil. When hot, carefully add the sage leaves and fry until crisp and glossy, about 1½ minutes total, flipping halfway through. Remove the skillet from the heat, lift the sage onto paper towels to drain, and sprinkle generously with salt.

Return the skillet to medium heat and add half the Brussels sprouts (cut sides down) and half the chestnuts. Sprinkle with salt. Cook, shaking the pan occasionally, until the undersides are deep, golden brown, about 4 minutes. Transfer to a large bowl. Add the remaining oil, Brussels sprouts, and chestnuts to the skillet and repeat.

Drain the currants and add them to the cooked sprouts. Crumble in half the fried sage leaves and toss through. Garnish with the remaining whole fried sage leaves. Add salt and pepper to taste.

Tip: Peeled and cooked chestnuts are widely available in the late fall and winter.

Celery

I have, in the past, maligned celery as relatively useless—useless for everything, in fact, but *mirepoix*, that cubic trio of celery, carrots, and onions that underpins soups and stews. I've allowed the stalks to wither and die, and have questioned, deeply, the sincerity of those who claim, without irony, that "Ants on a log is actually a really good snack." But recently I've changed my tune. Lo and behold, there's an enormous difference between fresh-from-the-farm celery and the prepackaged, bagged kind that languishes on grocery shelves. While the former is crisp, with barely noticeable strings and an audible snap, the latter is bendy and limp, with an off-putting bitterness and fibers that stick in your teeth.
Opt for shiny, spanking-new celery. When it begins to droop and lose its crunch, cook it, or peel off the fibers one by one and knit yourself a nice green sweater.
Tip: To dice, quarter celery sticks lengthwise, running the tip of your knife along their natural grooves. Bundle them up and slice crosswise to create perfect cubes.

SIMPLE USES FOR CELERY:

braised celery gratin = celery + butter + shallot + wine + stock + Gruyère + panko
stuffing = celery + onions + bread cubes + chestnuts + apples + sage + stock
salad = fennel + celery + cucumber + pomegranate seeds + grapes + lemon vinaigrette

Black Lentil Celery Couscous with Jeweled Fruit

Celery is used twice in this dish: softened in the beginning with a little olive oil, and tossed in at the end for a decisive crunch. You may substitute traditional couscous for the whole wheat and brown or green lentils for the black ones. (The black ones are especially pretty, though.)

•••••••••••••••••••••••••••••••••••••• SERVES 6 TO 8 ••••••••••••••••••••••••••••••••••••••

½ cup (100g) black beluga lentils, picked over and rinsed

2 tablespoons olive oil

1 small yellow onion, diced

1 large carrot, diced (about ½ cup)

4 stalks celery (no leaves), diced (about 2 cups)

Kosher salt and freshly ground black pepper

⅔ cup (110g) mixed dried fruit (any combination of cranberries, cherries, currants, golden raisins, apricots, figs, and/or dates), diced

½ teaspoon turmeric

1 cup (180g) whole-wheat couscous

Juice of 1 orange (about ¼ cup, or 60ml)

½ cup (60g) pistachios

Place the lentils in a medium saucepan with 1½ cups (355ml) cold water. Bring to a boil. Reduce the heat, cover, and simmer very gently until tender, 15 to 20 minutes. Drain. Transfer to a large serving bowl.

Meanwhile, place a large saucepan over medium heat and add the olive oil, onion, carrot, one-fourth of the celery (1 stalk, about ½ cup), ½ teaspoon salt, and ¼ teaspoon pepper. Sauté, stirring occasionally, until the vegetables are soft, 10 to 15 minutes. Add the dried fruit, 1 cup (237 ml) cold water, and the turmeric. Bring to a rolling boil. Stir in the couscous, remove from the heat, and cover for 5 minutes. Fluff with a fork. Drizzle with the orange juice. Scrape into the bowl with the lentils.

Stir in the pistachios and the remaining diced celery. Season with salt and pepper. (You'll need at least ¼ teaspoon more salt.) Serve hot, warm, or at room temperature.

Tip: May be made up to two days in advance and kept refrigerated. Bring to room temperature before serving.

Cucumbers

The relationship of cucumbers to pickles is like grapes to wine: it makes sense, sort of, but mostly it's magical.

Magical because there's little about a briny pickle plucked from a barrel that evokes a cucumber from a garden. The rough shape, I suppose, is the same, but the flavor is so different that magic must play a role.

Mostly, I toss cucumber rounds in salads, or chop and stir them through yogurt when making *tzatziki* or *raita*. Both refresh the palate more effectively than cool water or frosty root beer.

Sharon Tyler Herbst, in *The New Food Lover's Tiptionary*, wrote that the inside of a cucumber is always cooler than its surrounding environment.

Good to know. Next time I feel flush, I'm rubbing cucumber flesh on my body.

I have no plans to follow suit with a pickle.

Tip: Scraping out the seeds or even the seedless membrane running through cucumbers removes some of their moisture, keeping salads extra crisp.

SIMPLE USES FOR CUCUMBERS:

garlic dill pickles = cucumbers + garlic + pickling spice + vinegar + water + salt + sugar + dill

tzatziki = strained yogurt + cucumbers + garlic + olive oil + mint + lemon

green salad = mixed greens + cucumbers + peaches + candied lemon peel + lemon vinaigrette

Cucumber Halloumi Salad with Licorice Notes

Toasted fennel seeds and abundant fresh tarragon lend a licorice-y backdrop to this unique salad, which pairs cucumbers with seared Halloumi, a Cypriot cheese that can be browned or grilled without melting. You'll find the interplay of textures, flavors, and temperatures irresistible.

SERVES 4

2 teaspoons fennel seeds

4 (½-inch-thick or 1.25cm-thick) slices Halloumi cheese, blotted dry

1 tablespoon extra-virgin olive oil

2 teaspoons sherry vinegar

½ medium garlic clove, smashed and minced

Kosher salt and freshly ground black pepper

1 English cucumber, unpeeled, halved lengthwise

¼ cup (10g) loosely packed chopped fresh tarragon leaves

In a small, dry nonstick skillet, toast the fennel seeds over medium heat, shaking the skillet a few times, until fragrant, 2 to 3 minutes. Transfer to a small dish. Crank the heat to medium high, add the Halloumi, and brown on both sides, turning once, about 4 minutes total. Set aside to cool slightly.

Whisk the oil, vinegar, and garlic in a medium serving bowl. Season with salt and pepper.

Run a small spoon (a serrated grapefruit spoon works well) along the length of each cucumber half, making a tunnel and scraping out the seedless membrane. Slice the cucumber into 1/2-inch-thick (1.25 cm) half-moons. Add to the vinaigrette along with the tarragon and toasted fennel seeds. Tear the cheese into irregular pieces and toss on top.

Toss gently to coat. Adjust seasonings to taste, and serve immediately.

Edamame

I would prefer not to discuss the fact that edamame, young soybeans picked before maturity, have what is known as "soy pod hair," or that their Chinese name, *mao dao*, means "hairy bean." Let's just go with the Japanese translation: "beans from the branch."

Let's also praise their soothing taste and satisfying texture. Edamame's rich, almost fatty flavor is rounder and sweeter than that of other legumes, and its affinity for salt makes it difficult to stop eating. With a tender crunch, they're just like potato chips, but for the simple fact that they're potato free. Otherwise they're twins.

Personal preference dictates whether you favor edamame still in their pods or those that have been shelled. Either way, the vast majority are sold frozen, so plan to boil them until tender.

And think beyond the salt shaker in terms of seasoning. A sprinkle or two is fine, but edamame love other flavors, too, including garlic, chile, and sesame.

Tip: Try puréeing or mashing cooked edamame; they make a delicious, and extremely pretty, alternative to hummus.

SIMPLE USES FOR EDAMAME:

succotash = edamame + corn + red bell pepper + scallion
noodle bowl = edamame + shiitakes + tamari + garlic + ginger + soba noodles + lime
warm potato salad = edamame + fingerling potatoes + crispy shallots + French vinaigrette

Toasted Nori Edamame with Garlic-Chile Oil

Adding garlic, red chile, and toasted nori—a seaweed best known for wrapping sushi—
to a simple bowl of edamame ups this Japanese staple's sex appeal.
Don't be afraid of the chile. (Stalwarts may want to use two.)

•• **SERVES 4 TO 6** ••

1 pound (454g) frozen, shelled edamame, cooked according to package directions, drained, and rinsed under cool water

2 sheets nori (dried seaweed)

Kosher salt

½ teaspoon plus 1 tablespoon sesame oil, divided

2 large garlic cloves, sliced thinly

1 medium red chile, sliced into thin rings

Preheat the oven to 300°F (150°C). Pat the edamame dry and transfer to a serving bowl.

Lay the nori side by side on a baking sheet. Brush the top of one sheet lightly with water. Sprinkle with ⅛ teaspoon of salt and drizzle with ½ teaspoon of the sesame oil. Quickly top with the second nori, pressing gently to adhere. Set a second baking sheet directly on top to compress the sheets together. Transfer the whole apparatus to the oven for 15 minutes. Remove the top baking sheet and let the nori cool to room temperature.

Meanwhile, in a small skillet, combine the remaining tablespoon of sesame oil, the garlic, and the chile (including the veins and seeds). Fry gently over low heat, stirring occasionally, until the garlic crisps and turns golden, 6 to 8 minutes. Scrape the garlic-chile mixture into the edamame and season generously with salt, to taste. Crumble the nori on top in irregular shards. Serve immediately, at room temperature.

Tip: Find sheets of nori in Asian grocery stocks or the Asian foods aisle of well-stocked supermarkets.

Fava Beans

Favas are shy.

First, there's that cushiony pod they huddle inside like a blanket. Then, they're encased in a pale green shell. You need to boil those shells before sloughing off their skin, assuming you've first impaled it with a pointy fingernail.

Oh, but is it worth it! Once you do release the tender beans, you'll discover they look just like tiddlywinks, at which point you can play with them, or you can eat them. Or perhaps, if you're lucky and have a bit of extra time, you can do both.

Tip: In addition to working with fresh fava beans (also known as broad beans), you can also find canned favas (sold as *ful* in Middle Eastern shops) and dried ones, which must be soaked and boiled for at least an hour until tender. Experiment with all the varieties, as they each have something unique to offer.

SIMPLE USES FOR FAVA BEANS:

topping for crostini = puréed favas + basil oil + crispy garlic + Romano cheese

spring sauté = blanched favas + asparagus + snap peas + olive oil + goat cheese + pistachios

soup = favas + tortellini + stock + Asiago cheese + pepper

Warm Fava Shallot Couscous

With green favas, pearly couscous, and sweet shallots, this warming sauté is both comforting and light. (To make it more entréelike, toss in some feta and toasted pistachios.) Buy the freshest favas you can find as older beans can be starchy.

·· **SERVES 4 AS A SIDE** ··

1½ pounds (680g) fresh fava beans (in-pod weight)

1 cup (180g) Israeli (sometimes called pearl) couscous

¼ cup (60ml) extra-virgin olive oil

1 large shallot or 2 medium shallots, thinly sliced (1¼ cups)

Kosher salt and freshly ground black pepper

⅓ cup (75g) pitted Kalamata olives, sliced

1 lemon, zest removed in long squiggly strips, juice squeezed into a small bowl

2 tablespoons thinly sliced fresh mint leaves

Bring a large pot of water to a boil. Crack the fava pods and squeeze the beans into a bowl. Rinse. Boil the beans for 2 minutes; then remove with a slotted spoon to a colander and rinse again to cool. Transfer to a small bowl. Add the couscous to the same pot and boil until al dente, about 5 minutes, skimming any scum that rises to the surface. Drain; rinse briefly to prevent clumping.

While the couscous cooks, use your thumbnail to pierce each fava's outer shell. Squeeze the dark green inner beans into a bowl; discard the shells.

In a large skillet, warm the olive oil over medium-high heat until almost shimmering. Add the shallots, ¼ teaspoon salt, and a grinding of black pepper. Sauté until the shallots are golden brown and starting to crisp, 4 to 5 minutes, stirring frequently to prevent burning. Reduce the heat to very low, add the favas, and stir until warm and glossy, 3 to 5 minutes longer. Test one bean; it should be tender.

Add the couscous to the favas along with the olives and some of the lemon juice, to taste; stir until hot. Adjust the salt and pepper. Garnish with the mint and lemon zest.

Tip: Consider preparing this dish with a friend. It's nice to have company when you shuck the favas, as this can take a bit of time.

Fennel

Every recipe has a story.

Here's the fake/fun version: The first fennel I ever tasted grew in Liguria. I picked it on a cool morning, emboldened by two espressos. That afternoon, I brought it to a trattoria, where the chef paired it with oranges, onions, and capers in a simple salad. He then prepared the rest of my meal, first pressing ravioli from sheets of tender pasta, then stirring a pot of *ragu* on an ancient stove. I sipped prosecco and tried to look cute.

Here's the true/real version: If I didn't make an effort to buy unfamiliar vegetables like fennel, I'd always come home with carrots and potatoes. So one day I took the plunge, bought the crazy-topped bulb, and dragged it home. I lopped off its fronds, carved out its core, and shaved it wafer-thin. In went slices of sharp onion and juicy orange. A drizzle of oil, some briny capers, a shower of salt and pepper. There. Salad. Done.

Tip: Seek fennel bulbs with fresh, dilly fronds. Halve through the base, then remove the core with an inverted V-shaped cut.

SIMPLE USES FOR FENNEL:

basic oven roasted = fennel slices + olive oil + salt + pepper

mirepoix = fennel + carrots + onions (use the fennel as a celery alternative in soups and stews)

pasta = fennel + garlic + olive oil + chickpeas + ditalini + crushed red pepper

Fennel-Orange Salad

Fennel and orange are a classic combination, and by adding red onions and capers you scratch several major flavor itches at once: sweet, juicy, sharp, briny, aromatic. If you have a mandoline, fetch it.

SERVES 2 (MAY BE EASILY DOUBLED)

2 oranges

1 fennel bulb, trimmed, dilly fronds
  reserved for garnish

½ medium red onion

2 tablespoons capers, drained

Extra-virgin olive oil, coarse salt, and
  cracked pepper, for serving

Using a large, sharp knife, carefully remove the peel and white pith from the oranges. (For guidance, see the instructions on peeling a pomelo in the recipe for Maple Pomelo Parfaits on page 134.) Set your mandoline to medium thickness and slice the oranges into rounds onto a cutting board. Arrange on a large rimmed plate or in a shallow serving bowl.

Adjust the mandoline to its thinnest setting. Slice the fennel and arrange decoratively near the oranges. Repeat with the red onion. Spoon the capers nearby.

Drizzle the salad with olive oil and, if there's any pooled orange juice on your cutting board, stream it over the salad. Season lightly with coarse salt and cracked black pepper. Garnish with minced reserved fennel fronds.

Green Beans

A green bean should pop when you crack it in half. You should hear it. If it's mute, set it down, take a breath, and walk away. Do not purchase quiet beans.

Once you have your beans back home, break off the stems. Just break them off. If the queen is coming, or anyone titled or knighted, go ahead and slice them on the diagonal, thus *frenching* them. But I know in my house, the queen hasn't visited in a good long while, and thus I've taken to ripping off the little stemmy heads with my fingers. Will they all turn out perfectly uniform? No. Do I believe you should care? I think you can answer this question.

Green beans are also quite easy to grow yourself. I say this as someone who has grown green beans and is not what is commonly referred to as a "skilled gardener." But plucking off that first bean, and hearing that loud, satisfying pop, is enough to make me want to become a percussionist.

Tip: Green beans stand up well to advanced prep. Blanch them for a few minutes in boiling water, then shock them in ice water. Pat dry, wrap loosely in paper towels, and refrigerate the bundle in a zip-top bag. They'll stay crisp and bright for about two days.

SIMPLE USES FOR GREEN BEANS:

side = cherry tomatoes + blanched green beans + black olive tapenade + olive oil

stir-fry = green beans + garlic + peanut oil + chiles + sesame oil + soy sauce

salad = green beans + new potatoes + Dijon vinaigrette + chives

Green Beans with Smoky Pistachio Dust

This dish has it all: beauty, flavor, and a unique texture from the pistachio dust.
In our family, we eat the beans like French fries, not stopping until we've cleaned the bowl.
Sprinkle the extra dust over boiled potatoes, steamed cauliflower, or grilled asparagus.

························· **SERVES 4** ·························

1 pound (454g) green beans, rinsed, stem ends snapped

2 teaspoons olive oil

$^3/_4$ cup (90g) dry-roasted, unsalted pistachios, toasted and cooled completely

$^1/_2$ teaspoon smoked paprika, or to taste

Kosher salt and freshly ground black pepper

Fill a bowl with ice water.

Bring a medium pot of generously salted water to a boil. Drop in the green beans and boil until al dente, 2 to 3 minutes. Drain. Transfer the beans immediately to the ice bath to set their color and stop the cooking process. Drain again, pat dry, and transfer to a large bowl. Drizzle with the olive oil.

Combine the pistachios, smoked paprika, $^1/_2$ teaspoon salt, and $^1/_8$ teaspoon pepper in a food processor fitted with the metal blade. Process for 30 seconds, or until finely ground and reduced to "dust." Sprinkle $^1/_2$ cup (60g) dust (reserve the rest for future use) over the green beans, adjust seasonings, and serve at room temperature.

Tip: When grinding the pistachios, use a full-size food processor if you have one, as it will give you the finest, "dustiest" consistency. A mini chop is fine in a pinch but won't break the nuts down quite as much.

Honeydew

I suffer from Honeydew Anxiety Disorder. Definition: a pathological fear of bringing home a chalky, unsweet honeydew.

A perfect summer honeydew is so spectacular, with tender, perfumed flesh and refreshing, plentiful juice, it's quite alarming not knowing what lies in wait when you manhandle one at the market. *Will you be phenomenal?*, you ask your honeydew, caressing it like a crystal ball. *Or will you taste like drywall?*

Common practice for determining ripeness is to tap on the honeydew and listen for a thump, but I've discovered an easier solution: befriend the vendor at your local farmers' market or the produce manager at the supermarket. They know what they're doing, and have all kinds of top secret information. Let them pick you a good melon and guarantee its perfection. Then if they steer you wrong, you'll have someone else to blame.

Tip: When you do land a perfect honeydew, squirt it with lime juice. Trust me on this. The acidic shot amps up the honey flavor while delivering a counterbalancing kick. Seek out heavy fruit and store at room temperature for 3 to 4 days. Then refrigerate. Uncut honeydew will not soften, or become fragrant, when ripe.

SIMPLE USES FOR HONEYDEW:

mojito = honeydew + lime juice + simple syrup (sugar + water) + light rum
sorbet = honeydew + basil + honey
kabobs = honeydew + red and yellow watermelon + cantaloupe

Honeydew Salad with Poppy Seed Dressing

On my bookshelf at home, my copy of **The Silver Palate Good Times Cookbook** *by Julee Rosso and Sheila Lukins has a recipe for chicken salad with pale green fruit, and it's got a scribbled notation on it. "Excellent*" it says, though frankly, it's a little tough for me to tell if the handwriting is mine or my mother's. (I inherited the book when she passed away.) The combination of cucumber, honeydew, and green grapes, my springboard for this recipe, has enthralled me since I first ate that dish many years ago.*

SERVES 4

½ medium honeydew, seeded, flesh scooped with a melon baller

½ medium English cucumber, seed membrane scraped out, cut into half moons

½ pound (227g) seedless green grapes, cut in half (about 1½ cups)

Juice of ½ lime

1 teaspoon canola or olive oil

1 teaspoon water

1 teaspoon honey

1½ teaspoons poppy seeds

4 large fresh mint leaves, thinly sliced

In a large serving bowl, combine the honeydew, cucumber, and grapes. Whisk the lime juice, oil, water, honey, and poppy seeds in a small bowl or glass measuring cup, and pour over the honeydew mixture. (Scrape any stubborn poppy seeds onto the salad.) Top with mint, give a good stir, and serve immediately.

Tip: Serve this summery salad as a counterpoint to something spicy, like a curry.

Kale

Having never heard of a kale chip until a few years ago, I suddenly can't escape them. This leafy green has become a wildly popular alternative for those seeking crispy, healthful snacks they can make at home. You just drizzle the kale leaves with oil, season them up, and roast them in a moderate oven until crisp.

Of course, kale also has more longstanding traditional uses, tossed into soups (as I've done on the following page) and stews, or folded into hearty pastas. Across the globe, kale enjoys especially widespread popularity. Swedes plate kale beside their Christmas hams, the Irish mix it with mashed potatoes in *colcannon*, and a Japanese company even whirls kale juice into *aojiru*, a dietary supplement and health tonic.

If you'd rather eat your kale than drink it (though I have friends who enjoy it juiced), nothing should stop you. Toss lacinato kale in salads with bright, citrusy dressings, or fling it into pots of wintry minestrone.

Just don't denigrate it. With abundant nutrients, great flavor, and impressive versatility, kale is more than just a four letter word.

Tip: To cut, strip kale leaves from their stems, roll the leaves up like a (super-healthy, non-tobacco-y) cigarette, and slice thinly crosswise into ribbons. This is called a *chiffonade*.

SIMPLE USES FOR KALE:

kale Caesar salad = lacinato kale + shredded Parmesan + croutons + lemon vinaigrette
macaroni and cheese = pasta shells + roux + smoked Gouda + kale + breadcrumbs
spicy kale chips = kale + olive oil + salt + crushed red pepper

Green Noodle Soup with Kale, Beans, and Parmesan Crisps

*This beautiful, green-laden soup showcases dark and healthful lacinato kale,
which may also be called Tuscan, black, or dinosaur kale. Parmesan rounds
provide a chewy bite, and crushed red pepper lends a warming kick.*

························· **SERVES 6** ·························

2 tablespoons extra-virgin olive oil

1 small onion, diced

$1/2$ medium fennel bulb (no fronds), cored and diced

2 garlic cloves, minced

$1/4$ teaspoon crushed red pepper

Kosher salt and freshly ground black pepper

4 cups (0.95 liters) vegetable stock

2 bunches lacinato kale (about $3/4$ pound or 340g)

1 (15-ounce, or 450g) can navy or cannellini beans, drained and rinsed

4 ounces (115g) spinach linguini or fettuccini, broken into 2-inch lengths

$1^{1}/_{2}$ cups (120g) coarsely shredded Parmesan cheese (about 2 ounces), divided

In a large saucepot or Dutch oven, heat the oil over medium heat. Add the onion, fennel, garlic, crushed red pepper, $3/4$ teaspoon salt, and $1/2$ teaspoon black pepper. Sauté, stirring occasionally, until the vegetables soften and begin to brown, 8 to 10 minutes. Add the stock and 3 cups water. Bring to a boil.

Meanwhile, strip the kale leaves by "unzipping" them with a downward motion. Roughly chop the leaves. (Discard the stalks.) Add the kale, beans, and linguini to the pot. When the soup returns to a boil, lower the heat to medium and simmer until the pasta is tender, 8 to 15 minutes, depending on the type and brand.

While the soup cooks, make the Parmesan crisps. Heat a large, nonstick skillet over medium heat. For each crisp, drop 2 tablespoons of cheese into a little mound, making 6 rounds total. Cook the crisps undisturbed for about 5 minutes, or until they bubble, brown, and begin to solidify. Flip with a thin spatula and cook the other side 2 minutes longer. Remove the skillet from the heat, and let the crisps harden completely.

Stir half of the remaining cheese into the soup. Adjust seasonings (you'll need about more salt and plenty of pepper). Divide among six bowls, floating 1 Parmesan crisp in each. Pass the remaining cheese at the table.

Kiwis

If kiwis were clothing, they'd be crazy bohemian tie-dyed T-shirts. These emerald green or golden fruits are visual stunners, with teensy black seeds set in bright-colored flesh. Of course, you'd never know this unless you sliced one open. From the outside they look like stubbly brown eggs.

Native to China, kiwis (nicknamed "monkey peaches") eventually settled in New Zealand and were rechristened to honor that nation's fuzzy national bird.

With mild, creamy interiors redolent of strawberries and melon, kiwis do best flying solo, or at least in minimal company. Sure you can work them into complicated recipes, but why bother? With something this beautiful and balanced, go simple, go clean, or go home.

Tip: To speed ripening, set hard kiwis in a paper bag with ethylene-producing fruits, like apples or bananas.

SIMPLE USES FOR KIWIS:

kiwi strawberry yogurt = puréed kiwis + strawberries + Greek yogurt
dessert = pastry shell + pastry cream + sliced kiwi + blueberries + raspberries + honey drizzle
kid-friendly party bites = cubed kiwi + cubed honeydew + cubed cantaloupe + toothpicks

Kiwis, Oranges, and Dates, en masse

When throwing a big brunch, set out an eye-catching kiwi salad quietly and without fanfare. People will be impressed, though your work will have been minimal.

4 large kiwis (1 pound, or 454g), just ripe

3 navel oranges

8 Medjool or deglet noor dates, pitted and chopped

Grab a large (preferably white) platter. Slice off the stem ends of each kiwi, then peel with a vegetable peeler. Slice $1/8$ inch (0.3cm) thick. Slice the stem ends off each orange, then perch on a flat end. Holding your knife at an angle, sweep down the sides of the orange, hugging the fruit to remove the peel and white pith. Slice the oranges $1/8$ inch (0.3cm) thick.

Lay the kiwi and orange rounds on your platter, overlapping slightly and nestling any extra kiwi pieces along the border. Heap the dates in the center.

Tip: Sharpening your knife before cutting the kiwi will net you much neater slices.

Leeks

The French know many things: how to speak French, how to stuff chocolate bars into pastries, and how to prepare leeks. The key, as with many fundamentals of French cuisine, is to introduce the leeks to wine, cream, butter, and cheese, a quartet of highly effective seasonings that could even make wood shavings taste terrific.

Related to both onions and garlic, leeks bear more than a passing resemblance to overfed scallions, though they taste far milder. American home cooks are fond of them in potato-leek soup, but for many, the love affair ends there, which is a shame. With their lovely green color, gentle flavor, and affinity for eggs, vinaigrettes, lemons, and even apples, leeks deserve to break free from the bounds of the potato box. Given their large size, they'd probably appreciate the extra breathing room anyway.

Tip: Store leeks in a plastic bag in your crisper so their oniony perfume doesn't penetrate nearby vegetables. When ready to use, halve them and rinse well, teasing apart their layers and giving them a thorough, effective cleanse.

SIMPLE USES FOR LEEKS:

grilled leeks = quickly blanched leek halves + Italian vinaigrette + hot grill

breakfast strata = sautéed leeks + mushrooms + fontina + milk + cream + eggs + bread + thyme

warm salad = stock-braised leeks + Dijon mustard + red wine vinegar + olive oil + parsley

Gruyère-Crusted Leeks and Apples

This warming, delicious, luxurious tangled mess of leeks, apples, Gruyère, wine, and cream will transport you to both Switzerland and France. All that's missing is a baguette and a roaring fire, which I strongly encourage you to provide yourself.

SERVES 4

4 large leeks, white and light green parts only, quartered lengthwise

1 tablespoon butter

1 tablespoon olive oil

¼ teaspoon ground nutmeg

Kosher salt and freshly ground black pepper

¼ cup (60ml) dry white wine

¼ cup (60ml) vegetable stock

2 tablespoons heavy cream

1 medium Granny Smith apple, unpeeled, cored, halved, and thinly sliced

¾ cup (90g) packed shredded Gruyère cheese

Bring a medium pot of water to a boil. Set a large bowl of ice water nearby.

Rinse the leeks well under cool running water, spreading the layers to release any grit. Blanch in the boiling water for 2 minutes. Drain and then add to the ice water. Drain again and squeeze dry between paper towels.

Combine the butter and olive oil in a large ovenproof skillet over medium-high heat. When the butter melts, add the leeks and nutmeg. Season with salt and pepper. Sauté, turning occasionally with tongs, until the leeks begin to brown, about 5 minutes. Add the wine and stock, bring to a boil, then reduce the heat, cover, and simmer gently until very tender, about 5 minutes. Add the cream, up the heat slightly, and let bubble until thickened, about 4 minutes.

Tuck the apple slices among the leeks. Sprinkle with the Gruyère. Broil until the cheese melts and turns golden brown, 2 to 4 minutes, watching carefully. Serve immediately.

Limes

I would never order a glass of seltzer. That shows no imagination, no personality, no pizzazz. But I would order a glass of seltzer . . . with a twist of lime. Lime screams moxie! Pluck! Chutzpah!

Limes pack a full-on acidic punch. They force drinks, desserts, and tacos to feel more confident and have more zing. Serve a coconut-laced green curry without lime, and the food sits on your plate in a funk, no energy, even, to climb up on your fork. Spritz it with lime and it perks up so fast it shoots right down your throat.

Keep squirting lime in guacamole, on honeydew, and in Mexican beers and cocktails. And who says you can't add it to iced tea?

Maybe a lemon, but that's no surprise. No one wants to be out of a job.

Tip: As with lemons and oranges, roll your lime on the countertop with a firm palm to prep it for juicing. You'll get a higher yield.

SIMPLE USES FOR LIMES:

simple snack = corn tortillas + lime + chili powder + salt

taco salad = lime + shredded romaine + black beans + avocado + cotija cheese + charred corn

lime mousse with raspberries = lime + eggs + sugar + cream + raspberries

Tarragon Lime Green Tea

My sister, Julie, helped me conceive of this refreshing iced tea,
a new favorite with citrusy, herbal notes that makes us both feel fancy.
Boiling the water in a kettle speeds things up.

·· SERVES 8 ··

4 bags green tea

8 cups (2 liters) hot, just-boiled water

¼ cup (85g) honey

1 bunch fresh tarragon

4 limes, divided

Ice

Place the teabags and water in a large bowl or pot. Whisk in the honey until dissolved. Add 2 leafy tarragon sprigs. Squeeze in the juice of 3 of the limes and toss in the spent limes, too. Set aside to steep, off the heat and uncovered, for at least 10 minutes, or until desired strength. Discard the teabags. Cool to room temperature.

Pluck out the limes and herbs. (If not serving right away, refrigerate.)

Cut the remaining lime into 8 wedges.

Divide the tea among eight ice-filled glasses, garnishing each glass with a fresh tarragon sprig and lime wedge.

Peas

Snow peas, English peas, snap peas, adorable *petits pois*. Bright green peas are so cute I just want to squeeze them until they pop out of their shells and then smother them with, well, not much. Peas taste great au naturel, and if they're really fresh, even a dab of butter may be overkill. Shuck, eat, repeat. That's my philosophy.

Because fresh peas pop up only in warmer weather, frozen peas are a popular stand-in during cooler months. Happily, when quickly steamed, blanched, or microwaved, they lose little of their character and virtually none of their bright, perky color. Just don't overcook them.

Despite my love for peas without adornment, they do take well to unexpected flavors. Several years ago, I enjoyed English peas with toasted macadamias and white chocolate at Ubuntu, a vegetable-focused restaurant in Napa. I realized then and there that peas are open to living life on the edge.

If they could be paired with chocolate, they could certainly be paired with . . . tabbouleh. And so they were.

Tip: If you love pasta, keep in mind that peas enjoy nestling in shapes with cozy hallows, like little shells or orecchiette. I don't recommend peas with spaghetti, unless you're fond of chasing them around the house.

SIMPLE USES FOR PEAS:

quick cold side salad = almond oil + snap peas + Marcona almonds + sea salt

curry = peas + cauliflower + potatoes + onions + garlic + ginger + turmeric + coriander + yogurt

risotto = onion + butter + stock + wine + saffron + Arborio rice + peas + lemon

Green Pea Tabbouleh

Green peas join the traditional marriage of bulgur, herbs, and lemon in a springy twist on flavorful tabbouleh, a popular Middle Eastern salad. Serve immediately or marinate for several hours in the refrigerator. (And there's no shame in using frozen peas. Buy a one-pound bag.)

•• **SERVES 6** ••

¾ cup (70g) quick-cooking bulgur

1 cup (237ml) boiling water

Juice of 2 lemons (about 6 tablespoons), divided

1 large or 2 small bunches Italian parsley, thick stems trimmed and discarded, leaves and skinny stems finely chopped (about 2½ cups, or 100g loosely packed)

1 bunch mint, stems discarded, leaves finely chopped (about ½ cup, or 20g loosely packed)

4 scallions, trimmed, white and green parts finely chopped

3 cups (400g) fresh or frozen peas, lightly steamed, boiled, or blanched, rinsed under cool water

3 tablespoons extra-virgin olive oil

Kosher salt and freshly ground black pepper

Place the bulgur in a large serving bowl. Add the boiling water and the juice of 1 lemon (about 3 tablespoons). Let stand, uncovered, 1 hour.

Stir in the parsley, mint, scallions, and peas. Toss well. Add the olive oil, remaining lemon juice, 1 teaspoon salt, and ¾ teaspoon black pepper. Adjust seasonings to taste. Serve immediately, or refrigerate for several hours to chill and allow the flavors to marry.

Tip: If you can't find quick-cooking bulgur, prepare the bulgur according to package directions. Soaking and a longer cook time may be required.

Spinach

Other than, say, iceberg lettuce, spinach is the ideal starter green. It's a gateway, in many respects, to harder core leaves like kale, chard, or collards. Part of this is due to its relative mildness, and the fact that pre-washed baby varieties are sold in easy-to-grab bags. But mostly, spinach is simply more familiar, and therefore less startling to those who might have a heart attack if approached by mustards or escarole in a dark alley.

Me? I like them all: spinach for its versatility in both raw and cooked form, and its brasher green cousins to prove my mettle.

A worthy ambassador, spinach deserves our esteem, respect, and considerable gratitude. Thank you, spinach.

Tip: To clean, plunge full-leafed spinach in a deep bowl of cold water. Lift up into a colander, rinse and refill the bowl, and repeat until all the grit has vanished. Spin dry.

SIMPLE USES FOR SPINACH:

salad = torn spinach + red grapefruit + cucumber + avocado + sunflower seeds
creamed spinach = spinach + onions + olive oil + roux + milk + cream
Spanakopita = phyllo dough + onions + spinach + feta + egg + butter

Spinach Smoked Gouda Frittata with Tomatoes

This spinach-laden frittata with just a hint of smoky cheese comes together in minutes and offers ultimate time-of-day flexibility. Serve it morning, noon, or night with toast, roasted potatoes, and a little fruit. A last-minute dribble of balsamic vinegar delivers a subtle, acidic pop.

SERVES 2 TO 4

4 eggs

1 tablespoon heavy cream

Kosher salt and freshly ground black pepper

2 tablespoons extra-virgin olive oil

1 small shallot, diced

4 cups (packed) baby spinach leaves (5 to 6 ounces, 110 to 140g), rinsed and spun very dry

$\frac{1}{4}$ cup (30g) shredded smoked Gouda

1 medium tomato, sliced

Good balsamic vinegar, for serving

Set an oven rack 5 inches (12 cm) from the heat source. Flip on the broiler.

Whisk the eggs, cream, $\frac{1}{2}$ teaspoon salt, and $\frac{1}{4}$ teaspoon pepper in a medium bowl. Set aside.

Swirl the oil along the bottom and up the sides of a $9\frac{1}{2}$-inch (24cm) cast-iron or ovenproof, nonstick skillet. (You may use a pastry brush.) Set the skillet over medium-low heat, add the shallot, and sauté, stirring occasionally, until soft and translucent, about 5 minutes. Add the spinach, one handful at a time, turning with tongs so it wilts. Crank the heat and sauté for about 5 minutes, until the spinach weeps and its moisture then evaporates, tossing a few times. (You want it relatively dry.) Lower the heat again.

Add the egg mixture, cheese, and tomatoes and cook until the frittata is three-quarters set, about 5 minutes, tilting the skillet now and again so the runny eggs slide toward the edges.

Broil until puffy and browned, 3 to 5 minutes, watching carefully. Let cool for 5 minutes. Serve wedges warm or at room temperature, with balsamic vinegar for dribbling.

Swiss Chard

People avoid chard. They see it at the market, with its big, imposing leaves, and think: If I bring that home, it'll overrun the crisper and suffocate the carrots in their sleep. And that might be true, but only if your chard is unnaturally large and your carrots are unnaturally small.

Actually, you want these larger leaves for making stuffed chard, which is my favorite way to eat this pretty green vegetable that comes both in classic white, for an understated elegance, and high-impact reds and yellows for more festive occasions.

Some people, like my friend Caroline, favor a stuffing of brown rice, vegetables, and cheese, but I'm mad for polenta. It's so bright and pretty, and the golden filling is dashing against the bright green leaves.

Of course, chard can be prepared much more simply, sautéed with garlic and oil, for example, and speckled with vinegar. But some of us prefer theatricality. Is that so wrong?

Tip: Store chard in a plastic bag in the crisper drawer for 2 to 3 days. Don't neglect the stems: slice them and sauté until tender.

SIMPLE USES FOR SWISS CHARD:

roasted chard "chips" = chard leaves + olive oil + salt
basic sauté = olive oil + shallots + lemon + chard + pine nuts + raisins + vinegar
entrée = whole-wheat pasta shells + chard + garlic + ricotta + toasted walnuts + walnut oil

Polenta-Stuffed Chard with Bubbly Parmesan

These gorgeous green parcels, best eaten on a Sunday night in front of a fire, are both dramatic and comforting (think lasagna, but without the pasta, ricotta, or mozzarella). Buy the largest Swiss chard leaves you can find, and keep in mind that the polenta takes an hour to chill.

· SERVES 4 ·

Kosher salt

¾ cup (112g) dry polenta (coarse cornmeal)

1 tablespoon butter

1 cup (80g) packed grated Parmesan cheese, divided

Pepper

1¼ cups (300ml) your favorite marinara or tomato sauce, divided

8 very large leaves Swiss chard, swished in cool water

Coat a 9½-inch (24cm) square pan with cooking spray and line the bottom with parchment.

In a medium saucepan, bring 3 cups (72ml) water and 1 teaspoon salt to a boil. Whisk in the polenta and reduce the heat to a gentle gurgle. Cook until thick, 10 to 15 minutes, whisking occasionally. Remove from the heat and stir in the butter, half the cheese, and a generous pinch of black pepper.

Scrape the polenta into the prepared pan and smooth the top. Cool for 15 minutes at room temperature, then refrigerate until cold, at least 1 hour. (After 1 hour, cover with plastic wrap.) Unmold and cut into eight 4 x 2-inch (10 x 5cm) rectangles. Wipe the baking pan dry and spread ½ cup (118ml) of the marinara along the bottom.

Preheat the oven to 400°F (200°C) and bring a kettle of water to a boil. Have several layers of paper towels on hand.

Make a narrow, upside down V-shaped cut about halfway down each chard leaf to remove the thick central steam. Place the leaves in a large bowl and cover with boiling water. Let soften for 6 minutes. Remove to the paper towels and pat very dry.

To form the rolls, lay 1 chard leaf on a cutting board. Lay 1 polenta rectangle horizontally along the bottom of the leaf and spoon 1 teaspoon of marinara on top. Roll the leaf upwards burritolike, encasing the polenta, and transfer to the baking pan seam side down. Repeat, nestling the rolls next to one other. Spoon the remaining sauce on top and sprinkle with the remaining cheese.

Bake for 10 minutes, then slip under the broiler for 1 to 2 minutes to brown the cheese. Serve hot.

Watercress

Let's bring back the tea sandwich, that pinky out wonder on thin crustless bread.

Don't forget the watercress, a tea sandwich staple with an invigorating, peppery bite. The best news? Because it's vitamin rich, you'll have a fine excuse to down another scone with clotted cream.

Watercress perks up salads and can be subbed for, or partnered with, greens with a similar flavor profile, like arugula or dandelion. You can even toss it in stir-fries, a popular application in Chinese cookery.

So broaden your repertoire to include this oft-neglected mustard. (Yes, it's a mustard.) You'll be pleased at how quickly it rouses everything from egg salad to soft, creamy butter.

Tip: If watercress is too peppery for you, try upland cress instead. Its flavor is milder, and it makes a fine substitute in the Watercress Butter on page 226.

SIMPLE USES FOR WATERCRESS:

tea sandwiches = watercress + herbed cream cheese + mint + thin-sliced walnut bread
salad = watercress + roasted beets + blood oranges + candied hazelnuts + blue cheese
side = watercress + mashed potatoes

Watercress Butter

With hints of garlic and lemon, this emerald butter makes a stunning spread on simple crackers. Leftovers can be tossed through hot potatoes or noodles, or sliced on bread with cucumbers and mint.

··· MAKES A GENEROUS ³/₄ CUP ···

1 bunch watercress (8 ounces or 227g), thick stems trimmed

¼ pound (1 stick, or 113g) soft butter, at room temperature

Zest and juice of 1 lemon

½ teaspoon honey

1 garlic clove, rough chopped

Kosher salt and freshly ground black pepper

Crackers, for serving

Decide how many crackers you plan to serve. Pinch off a corresponding number of watercress leaves to use as a garnish and set aside.

In a food processor fitted with the metal blade, purée the butter, the remaining watercress, lemon zest, honey, and garlic. (Stop the machine once or twice to scrape down the sides.) Season with salt and pepper, keeping in mind the saltiness of your crackers.

Spread the butter on crackers. Sprinkle with the lemon juice. Garnish each cracker with a reserved watercress leaf.

Refrigerate any leftover butter, covered. (To use again, microwave on half power until slightly softened, about 15 seconds. Stir.)

Zucchini

Left to their own devices, zucchini would take over the world. They'd wrap around lampposts and stretch across seas. They'd climb up on mountains, burrow in foxholes, sprout up in deserts, and fly into space.

I say this as someone who inherits so much zucchini from friends each summer that I can't help but wonder where on earth it all comes from. Is there a parallel zucchini-producing universe we've yet to discover? It wouldn't surprise me.

I'm not complaining, of course. I love zucchini—except those so big they could club me to death. Some zucchini are bigger than my children.

The secret to cooking zucchini, I've found, is high heat. Give them a good sear in a sauté pan, or char them on a blazing hot grill, and you get their appealing flavor without turning them to mush.

Whatever you do, just don't let them steam in their own hot breath.

Tip: Very large zucchini can taste like packing material. Unless you're baking, opt for small or medium zucchini instead. For information on zucchini flowers (also called squash blossoms), see page 137.

SIMPLE USES FOR ZUCCHINI:

fritters = zucchini + salt + corn + flour + onions + water + oil + egg

zucchini bread = flour + baking soda + baking powder + eggs + oil + brown sugar + cinnamon + zucchini

side = zucchini + Parmesan + lemon + toasted walnuts

Grilled Zucchini and Arugula Sandwiches

*These simple yet substantial sandwiches make a terrific lunch or alfresco summer dinner,
or wrap them up and toss in a picnic basket. If you like your sandwiches
cheesy, double the goat cheese and spread it on all eight bread slices.*

.... SERVES 4 ....

4 tablespoons (2 ounces) soft goat cheese

1 teaspoon milk

2 teaspoons (packed) thinly sliced fresh mint leaves

2 medium zucchini (about 1 pound, or 454g), trimmed and halved crosswise

2 thick slices red onion

1 medium yellow bell pepper (8 ounces, or 227g), quartered

5$\frac{1}{2}$ tablespoons olive oil, divided

Kosher salt and freshly ground black pepper

8 slices sourdough sandwich bread

1 cup (21g) (packed) baby arugula

Preheat a clean grill (or ridged grill pan) for direct medium heat. In a small bowl, combine the goat cheese, milk, and sliced mint. Stir and set aside.

Slice the zucchini into $\frac{1}{4}$- to $\frac{1}{2}$-inch-thick (0.65- to 1.25cm-thick) strips. Place them on a rimmed baking sheet with the onion slices. Flatten the pepper quarters with your palm and add to the baking sheet. Brush about 2$\frac{1}{2}$ tablespoons of the olive oil on the vegetables, coating both sides. Sprinkle both sides generously with salt and pepper.

Arrange the bread on a second baking sheet. Brush with the remaining oil.

Grill the vegetables until dark grill marks appear, 3 to 5 minutes per side. (Keep an eye on the zucchini as it may finish cooking first.) As they're ready, return the vegetables to the baking sheet.

Grill the bread, oiled side down. Cook on one side only until grill marks appear, 2 to 3 minutes.

To make the sandwiches, spread about 1 tablespoon of the cheese mixture on the ungrilled side of 4 bread slices. Top each with one quarter of the zucchini, a few rings of red onion, one piece of bell pepper, and one quarter of the arugula. Top with the remaining bread slices. Cut in half and serve.

Tip: Grilling zucchini allows you to keep it relatively firm. Don't overcook it. You want to have a little crunch.

PURPLE & BLUE

Blackberries

Moderately astringent, deep purple, and filled with an antioxidant-rich pigment called anthocyanin, blackberries seduce and bully in equal measure. Pop a perfect-looking specimen in your mouth: it will either delight you with its sweetness or shock you with a tartness so unnerving you'll want to crawl into a pothole.

Ah, but those sweet ones! It's those honeyed, tender blackberries that make this very roulette worth playing. They're one of summer's ultimate prizes, whether perched beneath a sugar rain, lining a cereal bowl, or floating in a custard puddle.

More, perhaps, than any of its kind, blackberries should be tasted before purchase. Better yet, find yourself a neighbor's bush or U-pick farm, and pluck the wares yourself. Just be prepared to chuck your T-shirt when you're done. Picking berries without mussing your clothes is harder than peeling an orange one handed.

Tip: Eat blackberries quickly, before they have an opportunity to mold. Store them in a single layer on a paper towel–lined plate in the fridge. Rinse seconds before eating.

SIMPLE USES FOR BLACKBERRIES:

parfait = blackberries + vanilla frozen yogurt + crushed gingersnaps
jam = blackberries + agave nectar + lemon
trifle = macerated blackberries + mascarpone + cream + sugar + angel food cake

Blackberry-Lime Cornmeal Shortcakes

Juicy blackberries, fluffy cream and tender shortcakes collide in this cornmeal and lime-flecked twist on a summer classic.

•• **SERVES 4** ••••••••••••••••••••••••••••••••••••••

Shortcakes:

1 cup (125g) all-purpose flour

½ cup (40g) medium-grind cornmeal

2 teaspoons baking powder

¼ teaspoon kosher salt

3 tablespoons granulated sugar

2 teaspoons finely grated lime zest

4 tablespoons unsalted butter, frozen until hard

½ cup plus 1 tablespoon (120ml) cold heavy cream

1½ teaspoons Demerara sugar, for sprinkling

Filling:

4 cups (440g) fresh blackberries

¼ cup plus 1 teaspoon (65g) granulated sugar, divided

1 tablespoon fresh lime juice

1 cup (237ml) cold, heavy cream

Additional lime zest, for garnish

Preheat the oven to 375°F (190°C). Line a baking sheet with parchment.

To make the shortcakes: In a large bowl, whisk the flour, cornmeal, baking powder, salt, granulated sugar, and zest. Using the large holes on a box grater, grate the butter over the dry ingredients. Fluff gently with a fork. Drizzle with the ½ cup (118ml) of the cream. Stir with a wooden spoon just until the ingredients cohere and no visible floury bits remain.

Transfer the dough to a floured board and form into a 4½-inch (11.5cm) diameter, 1-inch (2.50cm) high disc. Cut into quarters and transfer to the baking sheet. Brush with the remaining tablespoon of cream and sprinkle with the Demerara sugar. Bake the shortcakes until golden, risen, and firm to the touch, 18 to 20 minutes. Transfer to a rack to cool completely. Cut in half horizontally.

To make the filling: Toss the blackberries with ¼ cup (62g) of the sugar and the lime juice. Transfer half of this mixture to a small bowl and set aside. Take a potato masher to the remaining blackberry mixture and mash until pulpy. In a large bowl, whip the cream to soft peaks with the remaining 1 teaspoon of sugar.

To assemble: Lay 1 shortcake bottom on a plate. Dollop with some whipped cream, top with a few whole berries, replace the shortcake cap, and spoon some of the mashed blackberry pulp on top. Garnish with lime zest. Repeat with the remaining shortcakes, berries, cream, and zest. Serve immediately.

Tip: Grating frozen butter into the dry ingredients yields flaky shortcakes without the need for a pastry blender.

Blueberries

Who needs a tooth fairy? Give me a blueberry fairy instead. In her shiny, iridescent tutu she'd be a cross between Glinda and Tinkerbell. She'd flit about, all levity and grace, cradling a wee basket of perfect summer berries in her slender fairy arms. You'd wake up in the morning, grab a bowl, pour your cereal, and *whoa*! Where did *those* come from?! You'd griddle some pancakes, turn to fetch the syrup, and *shazam*, more berries! You'd whir a cake batter, prepare to slide it towards the oven, when, in an instant, blueberries would appear out of nowhere, raining down like a summer storm.

The recipe for Blueberry Nutmeg Cake that follows is a close adaptation of Marian Burros's Plum Torte, a recipe originally published in the *New York Times*. While I adore the plum version, I actually prefer this blueberry version even more. Why? Given blueberries' diminutive size, you can pile them on with irresponsible, reckless abandon.

Tip: Enjoy frozen blueberries guilt free in the off-season. I prefer the tiny wild ones from Maine. Just don't thaw them before adding to batters unless you're fond of purple streaks.

SIMPLE USES FOR BLUEBERRIES:

breakfast = blueberries + nectarines + yogurt + crêpes
beverage = blueberries + kiwi + honey + seltzer
sauce = blueberries + sugar + lemon + water

Blueberry Nutmeg Cake

This cake's appeal lies not only in its ease of preparation, but in its simple, glorious presentation. I tip my hat to Marian Burros for creating the original plum torte that inspired my twist. This cake tastes especially amazing when baked one day ahead.

·················· **SERVES 8** ··················

2 cups (220g) blueberries

³/₄ teaspoon lemon juice

³/₄ cup plus 2¹/₂ tablespoons (190g) granulated sugar, divided

1 cup (125g) all-purpose flour

1 teaspoon baking powder

³/₄ teaspoon ground nutmeg, divided

¹/₄ teaspoon kosher salt

¹/₄ pound (1 stick, or 113g) unsalted butter, at room temperature

2 eggs

Preheat the oven to 350°F (175°C). Grease a 9-inch (23cm) springform pan and line the bottom with parchment.

In a medium bowl, toss the blueberries with the lemon juice and 1 tablespoon of the sugar. In a separate bowl, sift the flour, baking powder, ¹/₂ teaspoon of the nutmeg, and the salt.

Using an electric mixer, cream the butter and ³/₄ cup (187g) of the sugar on medium-high speed until light and fluffy, about 3 minutes. Add the eggs, 1 at a time, beating well after each addition. Scrape down the sides of the bowl. With the mixer on low, beat in the sifted ingredients. Do not overbeat. Scrape into the prepared pan and smooth the top.

Scatter the berries and any juices over the batter. Stir the remaining 1¹/₂ tablespoons of sugar and the remaining ¹/₄ teaspoon of nutmeg together and sprinkle over the berries. Bake in the center of the oven for 50 to 60 minutes, or until a skewer comes out clean and the cake just begins to pull away from the sides. Cool in the pan for 30 minutes.

Spring the cake free, then finish cooling completely. Slide a wide, thin spatula under the cake to transfer it to a large plate. Wrap tightly with plastic and let mellow at room temperature for several hours, or overnight, before eating.

Tip: While the cake may appear dry when freshly baked, it takes on a fantastic dampness after an overnight rest, and continues to improve with age. (The blueberries become almost jammy as the cake matures.) After 24 hours, I store any leftovers, tightly wrapped, in the fridge.

Eggplant

Prepared wrong, eggplant can be an oily, sloppy mess. Prepared right, it can satisfy hunger like few other vegetables.

Meaty eggplant shines in world cuisines, from Asian stir-fries and Middle Eastern baba ghanouj to French ratatouille and Italian eggplant parm. Roasted long and slow on the grill or in a hot oven, this pretty member of the nightshade family collapses, almost puréeing itself. If only it would do the laundry.

One final word on eggplant: garlic.

Tip: Salting eggplants used to be *de rigeur*, but I rarely bother. Because I don't fry it, I've never found the extra moisture to be a problem.

SIMPLE USES FOR EGGPLANT:

baba ghanouj = eggplant + garlic + lemon + tahini + oil + smoked paprika + mint
stir-fry = eggplant + oil + garlic + sugar + soy sauce + vinegar + sherry
bruschetta = toasted French bread + garlic-roasted tomatoes + grilled eggplant rounds

Eggplant Romesco Rigatoni

Romesco is a traditional Catalan sauce with nuts, tomatoes, bell peppers, and fried bread,
but here I offer my eggplant version. It makes a hearty sauce for rigatoni, or you can
skip the pasta altogether and serve it as a dip or high-impact sandwich spread.

·· **SERVES 6** ··

2 dried pasilla or ancho
  chile peppers

1 globe eggplant (about 1 pound, or
  454g), unpeeled, cut in large dice

2 medium red bell peppers, cut in
  large dice

½ medium red onion, quartered

2 garlic cloves, peeled

2 tablespoons plus 2 teaspoons
  extra-virgin olive oil, divided,
  plus additional for drizzling

Kosher salt and freshly ground
  black pepper

1 (14.5-ounce, or 420g) can whole
  peeled tomatoes

⅓ cup (75g) whole almonds

1 slice country-style or sourdough
  bread

½ cup (20g) minced fresh Italian
  parsley

1 pound freshly cooked rigatoni,
  ½ cup (118ml) of pasta water reserved for serving

Preheat the oven to 400°F (200°C).

Set the dried chiles in a bowl and add boiling water just to cover. Weight with a small ramekin to keep the chiles submerged. Set aside.

Place the eggplant, bell peppers, onion, and garlic on a rimmed baking sheet. Drizzle with 2 tablespoons of the oil, 1 teaspoon salt, and ½ teaspoon black pepper. Rub the seasonings in with your fingers. Spread the vegetables in a single layer.

Dump the tomatoes and their juices in a medium baking dish. Set both the baking sheet and the baking dish on separate oven racks and roast until the eggplant and peppers have browned, about 30 minutes, stirring everything twice. Remove everything from the oven and reduce the temperature to 350°F (175°C).

Allow the eggplant mixture to cool for 5 minutes, then scrape into the bowl of a food processor fitted with the metal blade. Place the almonds and the bread on the same baking sheet and brush the bread on both sides with the remaining olive oil. Toast in the oven, flipping the bread halfway through, about 8 minutes total. Break the bread into pieces.

While the bread and nuts cool, drain, stem, seed, and rough-chop the chiles and add them to the food processor. Add the nuts, bread, and tomatoes with any residual juices as well. Purée until smooth. Serve with hot rigatoni, adding a bit of pasta water (1 tablespoon at a time) to thin the sauce, if desired, and garnishing each portion with parsley and a final drizzle of olive oil.

Figs (Mission)

Fig trees are essentially jam trees. As the heavy fruits ripen, they hang low, soften, and warm in the sun, and if you're ever fortunate enough to grab them from a tree yourself, you'll want to have some toast nearby. Fresh ricotta wouldn't hurt either.

Sweet Mission figs (sometimes called Black Mission figs) sport royal colors inside and out, with deep red interiors and thin purple skins. Cooked, they ooze and melt: simply brush them with oil, then broil or grill them for a minute or two. Drizzle with cream.

Don't feel like cooking? No problem. Set an army of halved figs on a platter, press bits of soft chèvre or Gorgonzola into their bodies, and drizzle them with syrupy balsamic. Scatter on some toasted pistachios and go sit alone in the sun. You don't even need a spoon.

Or hold whole figs by their nubby stems and eat the fruit in ways that might embarrass the elderly, teenagers, religious officials, or passersby.

Shall I continue?

Tip: Figs are delicate and won't last long. Keep them refrigerated, do not jostle them, and eat them quickly.

SIMPLE USES FOR FIGS:

crostata = pie dough (*pâte brisée*) + almond frangipane + halved figs + honey

starter over greens, or dessert = oven-baked figs + toasted walnuts + manchego + aged balsamic

pizza = pizza crust + mozzarella + figs + arugula + olive oil

Fig and Wheat Berry Salad with Blue Cheese

When fresh Mission figs show up in markets, make this pretty and filling purple grain salad. In the off season, substitute dried figs for the fresh. (You won't get the same bold color contrast, but it will still be delicious.)

································ **SERVES 6 AS A SIDE OR 4 FOR LUNCH** ································

3 cups (470g) cooked wheat berries (see Tip below)

½ pound (227g) mesclun (about 6 cups), loosely packed

¾ pound (340g) Mission figs (about 14 figs), stemmed and quartered

3 tablespoons olive oil

2 tablespoons balsamic vinegar

2 teaspoons honey

Kosher salt and freshly ground black pepper

¼ cup (40g) blue cheese crumbles

¼ cup (30g) toasted, chopped pecans, optional

Place the cooked, cooled wheat berries in a large, shallow serving bowl. Toss in the mesclun. Lay the figs decoratively on top. In a small bowl or glass measuring cup, whisk the oil, vinegar, and honey. Season to taste with salt and pepper. Drizzle half over the salad and toss through. Sprinkle with the cheese and pecans, if using. Toss again, taste, and add additional dressing, 1 tablespoon at a time, until it reaches your desired level of flavor and moistness. Serve immediately, at room temperature, passing any additional dressing alongside.

Feel free to substitute arugula, mixed herbs, torn lacinato kale, or even baby spinach for the mesclun.

Tip: To cook wheat berries, soak 2 cups (224g) hard red winter wheat berries for several hours or overnight. (I generally skip this step, but it purportedly eases digestion.) Strain, place in a deep saucepan, add 1 teaspoon salt, cover with 7 cups (2 liters) cold water, and bring to a boil. Reduce heat and cook at a steady simmer, covered, for about 1 hour, or until al dente. Drain and rinse. (Freeze any you don't use in the salad.)

Plums

It's exceedingly difficult to choose favorites from the produce kingdom,
as the fear of offending is high. Who could pick between a cherry and a peach? Who'd praise
a pea in the presence of a fava? If a watermelon caught you flirting with a honeydew, all hell
would break loose.

And yet, my affection for plums is intense. It's immoderate. It may even be untoward. When
the ragged edge of my tooth pricks a plum's shiny, taut skin, I don't quite hear angels sing,
but I don't *not* hear them sing. Are you feeling me?

The best plums, to my mind, are purple skinned, with juicy, sangria-colored flesh. I like
other kinds, too—all kinds, in fact—but it's the darkest ones I favor most.
If I favored anything. Which of course I don't.
Tip: When buying plums, I always err on the harder side. An overripe plum is sad.

SIMPLE USES FOR PLUMS:

salad = sliced plums + ricotta salata + frisée + balsamic
breakfast = stewed plums + barley + milk + pistachios
dessert = plums + cherries + mascarpone + kirsch

Purple Cabbage

He was Cabbage, and I was Bean Paste. As Peace Corps Volunteers in Eritrea, a small East African country, my husband and I accepted the nicknames with resigned humor. Cheryl sounded close enough to *shero*, the Tigrinya word for a local staple of spiced puréed chickpeas, and the name Colin approximated *cowlo*, or cabbage. So for two years as eighth and ninth grade English teachers, we responded to daily calls of *Memher Shero* (Teacher Bean Paste) and *Memher Cowlo* (Teacher Cabbage). We would approach the school each day, and the children would call: Bean Paste is coming! Cabbage is coming!

I guess it could have been worse. Fact is, Eritreans love their cabbage and shero, two dietary staples they eat with *injera*, a spongy, fermented flatbread the size of a bathmat.

Good thing our names weren't close to *injera*. *Spongy Fermented Flatbread is coming!* doesn't have nearly the same ring.

Tip: Winter cabbage is known for its longevity and will remain fresh for several weeks in the fridge.

SIMPLE USES FOR PURPLE CABBAGE:

alitcha = oil + cabbage + potatoes + carrots + onions + garlic + ginger + turmeric + water (approximation of an Eritrean stew)

stuffed cabbage = blanched cabbage + brown rice + shiitake mushrooms + onions + canned tomatoes

coleslaw = red and Napa cabbage + carrots + buttermilk + mayo + cider vinegar + mustard

Peanut-Strewn Purple Cabbage Slaw

I'm actually a big fan of traditional, creamy coleslaw, but I sometimes crave a different flavor profile. Here, purple cabbage joins forces with apples, carrots, and red onion, and the colorful mess gets capped with crunchy, protein-filled peanuts. It's not just slaw; it's lunch.

•• **SERVES 4 TO 6** ••

Juice of 2 medium oranges (about $\frac{1}{2}$ cup, or 120ml), divided

1 medium crisp, red apple (like Fuji), unpeeled, cored, and quartered

1 small or $\frac{1}{2}$ medium head purple cabbage (about 1 pound, or 454g total), cored, quartered

1 large carrot, peeled

$\frac{1}{4}$ small red onion, very thinly sliced (about $\frac{1}{4}$ cup, or 40g)

3 tablespoons extra-virgin olive oil

Kosher salt and freshly ground black pepper

1 cup (150g) roasted, unsalted peanuts, finely chopped

Pour half the orange juice (about $\frac{1}{4}$ cup, or 60ml) into the bottom of a large serving bowl.

Using the medium shredding disk on a food processor, shred the apple and scrape it into the serving bowl. Toss well so the juice coats the apple. Shred the cabbage and carrot together next, and scrape into the bowl along with the sliced onion.

In a separate, small bowl, whisk 3 tablespoons of the remaining orange juice with the olive oil. Season generously with salt and pepper. Drizzle over the slaw, add half the peanuts, and stir to combine.

Mound the remaining peanuts on top. Sprinkle with the remaining tablespoon of orange juice and serve immediately.

Tip: If making ahead, store the apples with the vinaigrette in one container and the rest of the slaw (except the peanuts) in another. Combine with the peanuts just before serving.

Grapes

I used to wander the farmers' market quietly, drinking in the sights and sounds, but keeping to myself. What's that weird vegetable? Beats me. I'd quickly move on.

But in the past few years, I've changed. In a world where people text but don't talk and tweet but don't greet, the market is a great social beehive where eaters and growers can actually collide. If only we shoppers make the effort.

Now, I chat every weekend with Donna and Grace. Donna sells beautiful artichokes and sweet winter squash. Grace sells buckets of grapes and pistachios fresh from the tree. We talk, and they teach me—what to look for and how to prep it; they offer fresh ideas, and simple recipes.

Look, I'll be the first to admit that purple grapes taste sweet whether you've met Grace or not. But these small weekly moments, these brief conversations, make those grapes mean more. At least, they mean more to me.

Tip: If you ever have a chance to taste *rogig*, you should. Made from walnuts, cornstarch, and boiled grape juice, this Armenian candy hangs and cures for several days before being rolled in powdered sugar. Grace introduced it to me.

SIMPLE USES FOR GRAPES:

grape Waldorf salad = apples + purple grapes + celery + walnuts (mayo optional)

fruit salad = halved purple grapes + halved mission figs + purple plum wedges + blackberries

world's simplest snack = frozen grapes

Grape Fontina Rosemary Skewers

Grapes and rosemary are a classic Italian duo (con l'uva al rosmarino). *Here, they're threaded on rosemary skewers with marinated Fontina for a perfect party bite. Allow 4 hours for the cheese to marinate.*

MAKES 24 SKEWERS

24 rosemary sprigs

³/₄ teaspoon crushed red pepper

2 tablespoons white wine vinegar

2 tablespoons extra-virgin olive oil

Kosher salt

¹/₂ pound (227g) fontina cheese, red wax removed, cheese cut into 24 (³/₄-inch or 2cm) cubes

48 purple grapes (about 2 cups, or 300g)

Strip the bottom half of each rosemary sprig clean of its needles. Mince enough of the needles to measure ¹/₂ cup, loosely packed. (Reserve the remaining needles for another use.) Place the sprigs in a plastic bag and refrigerate until ready to use.

In a small bowl, whisk together the minced rosemary, red pepper, vinegar, and oil. Season lightly with salt. Transfer to a quart-size zip-top bag and add the cheese. Squeeze out the air, close the bag, and refrigerate for 4 hours, massaging and turning the bag once or twice if you're able.

To form the skewers, thread 1 grape, then 1 marinated cheese cube, then another grape on the bottom of each rosemary sprig. Place on a platter, cover lightly, and let stand for 20 minutes. Serve at room temperature.

Tip: You can also substitute cherry tomato–sized *ciliegine*, little balls of mozzarella packed in water, for the fontina. Buy 1 (8-ounce or 237ml) container, which has about 24 pieces.

Red Leaf Lettuce

With its autumnal-looking leaves, red leaf lettuce makes a dramatic addition to the salad bowl. While it doesn't offer the same strong taste as radicchio, or the same eau de parfum as certain cabbages, that's a feature, not a bug. In fact, its very charm lies in its ability to deliver frilly texture, impressive nutrients, and pretty color without an assertive flavor of its own.

Use the floppy leaves for lettuce wraps, folding them around skinny rice vermicelli seasoned with scallions, carrots, ginger, and soy. Just don't overfill them; these leaves are quite tender and may tear if overburdened.

Or keep things ultra simple: pair red leaf lettuce with foods in complementary shades. Crimson grapes and edible flowers, for instance, make the daintiest of salads, with red leaf lettuce happily occupying center stage.

Tip: Red leaf lettuce doesn't store well. Buy it in small quantities, keep refrigerated, and use within two or three days.

SIMPLE USES FOR RED LEAF LETTUCE:

salad = red leaf lettuce + clementine + radish + golden raisins + walnut oil

lettuce wraps = red leaf lettuce + jicama + carrots + crushed peanuts + cilantro + marinated tofu

sandwich = pita + red leaf lettuce + falafel + tahini + cucumber

Red Leaf Lettuce Salad with Grapes and Flowers

Say you're cooking a big meal that calls for a light but showy salad.
Here's one with a huge visual punch that takes twelve seconds to throw together,
and that's if you've got one hand tied behind your back. Otherwise, it's quicker.

· **SERVES 4** ·

¼ cup (60ml) extra-virgin olive oil

¼ cup (60ml) balsamic vinegar

¼ teaspoon honey

Kosher salt and freshly ground black pepper

1 medium head red leaf lettuce, leaves separated but left whole

2 cups (300g) seedless red grapes, halved

1 (³⁄₄-ounce or 21.5g) package edible flowers, such as borage, calendula, geraniums, marigolds, nasturtium, and pansies

Coarse salt, optional

In a medium bowl, whisk the oil, vinegar, and honey together until emulsified. Season with salt and pepper.

Place lettuce leaves in a large salad bowl. Sprinkle in the grapes.

Just before serving, moisten the salad with a few tablespoons of the vinaigrette, tossing to coat lightly. Garnish with the flowers and sprinkle with coarse salt (if using). Serve immediately, passing the remaining vinaigrette alongside.

Red Onions

A vegetarian sandwich needs several things: avocado for creaminess, plus sprouts, cucumber, and definitely red onion for crunch. You want to put cheese on there? Fine. Hummus is good, too, if you delete the apple and replace it, maybe, with some roasted red peppers or marinated eggplant.

But the red onion is key. Thin slivers wake up the palate and provide a jolt, a spark that cuts through the richness of creamy or fatty ingredients, ingredients that coat the tongue or settle on the roof of your mouth. Without the red onion, your mouth might glue shut, and then how will you finish your sandwich?

Of course, red onions can also be gently and lovingly warmed in a bit of oil, spiced and sugared and vinegared until they melt in a slippery, sweet-and-sour sea. This glistening jam can settle onto a piece of crisp bread, or be spooned, slowly and with care, into a bowl of warm, soothing dal.

Tip: Theoretically, eating parsley combats onion breath.

SIMPLE USES FOR RED ONIONS:

red onion rings = onions + beer batter (flour + beer + paprika + salt and pepper) + oil
sandwich = bagel + vegetable cream cheese + slivered red onions + sprouts + cucumbers
mixed grill = red onions + red peppers + Portobello caps + olive oil

Curried Red Onion Jam with Simple Dal

A dal is an Indian pulse porridge, often made with lentils.
*This version starts out quite humble. Then a dollop of glistening red onion jam
adds a lusty note right at the end. Save any leftover jam for sandwiches.*

•••••••••••••••••••••••••••••••••••• **SERVES 4 TO 6** ••••••••••••••••••••••••••••••••••••

2 tablespoons butter

1 tablespoon vegetable oil

3 medium red onions, diced

Kosher salt and freshly ground
    black pepper

⅓ cup (67g) packed dark
    brown sugar

1 tablespoon curry powder

¼ cup (60ml) cider vinegar

2 cups (350g) red lentils, picked
    through and rinsed

2 tablespoons minced fresh ginger

½ to 1 whole small red chile
    pepper, seeded (if desired) and
    minced, or to taste

2 star anise pods

Set the butter and oil in a large skillet over medium heat. Add the onions, 1 teaspoon salt, and ½ teaspoon pepper. Sauté, stirring occasionally, until softened and translucent, about 10 minutes.

Stir in the brown sugar, curry powder, and vinegar. Let bubble for a few seconds, then reduce the heat to low. Cook until thick and jammy, 30 to 40 minutes, stirring occasionally.

Meanwhile, set the lentils, ginger, chile, star anise, and 6¾ cups (1.5 liters) cold water in a medium saucepan and bring to a boil. Reduce the heat to a gentle simmer and cook 30 to 40 minutes, uncovered, until thick, loose, and porridgelike, stirring occasionally and adding 1½ teaspoons salt and ¾ teaspoon pepper halfway through. (Dal will thicken a bit upon standing.) Adjust the seasonings one final time, to taste, and discard the star anise.

Divide the dal among serving bowls. Spoon a generous scoop of red onion jam (re-warm if necessary) on top. (Refrigerate any leftover jam.)

Tip: For a more filling meal, spoon this dal over brown rice.

WHITE

Bosc Pears

If there's one pear variety you can afford to overbuy, it's the crisp, hard Bosc. True, it lacks the juiciness of an Anjou and the dramatic coloring of a Red Bartlett, but a Bosc pear is always dependably crunchy and sweet. It seems to last forever in the crisper, too, and if you happen to forget it's there and unearth it a few weeks later, you can actually hit it with a hot oven and roast it back to life. Try that with an overripe Bartlett. (Actually, don't. It will turn into mush.)

Boscs are so good raw when paired simply with a hunk of Stilton or Cheddar, it's easy to forget how many different ways you can abuse them with heat. My favorite way is to give them a hard sear in buttery caramel. They wear the sweet glaze like a coat, pulling it close so it warms and sweetens in equal measure. Whether you splash them with cream, sink them in batter, or splay them atop a big bowl of oatmeal, sautéed Boscs manage to be both rustic and elegant.

Tip: To check a Bosc for ripeness, press the elongated area beneath the stem. It should give just a little. Then you can transfer it to the fridge.

SIMPLE USES FOR BOSC PEARS:

poached pears = small whole peeled Bosc pears + sugar + water + red wine + cinnamon stick

salad = Bosc pears + escarole + buttermilk dressing (buttermilk + mayo + sour cream + lemon + garlic) + chives + walnuts

sandwich = sliced Bosc pear + arugula + red onion + chutney + Cheddar + flatbread

Warm Honey-Spice Pears over Steel-Cut Oatmeal

As soon as the rain comes and the mercury dips, I reach for the oats.
Steel-cut oats are especially hearty, and when you top them with sweet, warm,
honeyed pears, you've got a breakfast that soothes you right to your bones.

SERVES 4

4 cups (1 quart, or 0.95 liters) milk, cold water, or a combination

1 cup (90g) steel-cut oats

2 tablespoons butter

2 tablespoons honey

½ teaspoon ground ginger

¼ teaspoon ground cinnamon

3 medium unpeeled, firm Bosc pears, cored, stemmed, and cut into eighths

In a medium (3 to 4-quart or 3 to 4-liter) saucepan, bring the milk (or water) slowly up to a boil. Once it starts bubbling, stir in the oats, and reduce the heat to medium low. Let bubble gently but steadily, uncovered, for 25 to 30 minutes, stirring occasionally. (If a milk skin forms, stir to dissolve.) Remove from the heat and let stand for 10 minutes to thicken.

Meanwhile, place a large, wide skillet over medium-high heat. Add the butter, honey, ginger, and cinnamon. When the butter melts and starts to sizzle, stir it quickly with a heatproof spatula to combine with the honey and spices and swirl the pan a few times. Add half the pears, cut sides down, and move them around in the sauce to coat. Cook undisturbed for 5 to 10 minutes, or until the bottoms turn golden brown. Flip with tongs, and cook the other side for 5 to 10 minutes longer, or until browned. Remove the pears to a plate. Add the remaining pears to the caramel and repeat. (The caramel will darken during the cooking process; make sure it doesn't burn.) Keep the pears warm.

Give the oats a good stir and divide among four bowls. Top with the pears, and serve.

Tip: I find the sweetness of the pears is sufficient to sweeten my oatmeal, but by all means, doctor your oatmeal to your liking.

Cauliflower

As a brassica—or a member of the mustards or cabbage family—cauliflower is of hearty stock, a vegetable that can stand up to a blanket of cheese, a spicy curry, or an extended soak in a pickly brine. Just don't overcook it; its character lies, at least in part, on its decisive crunch.

Ivory and sophisticated, it acts as a calm visual counterpoint to more riotous vegetables across the color wheel. Blanch the florets and offer them as crudités with jicama, mushrooms, and even white asparagus. Served with a creamy white dip, even a bride could eat them without sullying her gown.

Or ignore that advice and toss it in a stir-fry. Cauliflower never whines about a quick turn in a hot pan.

Tip: Consider cutting cauliflower florets smaller than you normally might. Unlike broccoli, whose florets fall apart if you snip them too close to the top, cauliflower tips retain their shape when cut teeny tiny; plus, they'll cook a whole lot faster. Eat the stalks as you work.

SIMPLE USES FOR CAULIFLOWER:

curry = sautéed cauliflower + onion + garlic + ginger + curry powder + Greek yogurt
cauliflower and cheese = roasted cauliflower + roux + Cheddar cheese
side = steamed cauliflower + hazelnuts + brown butter

Ginger Cashew Cauliflower

Cut each piece of cauliflower into tiny florets. Use a small, sharp paring knife, and take your time. The rest of the recipe goes quickly. For a complete meal, serve with cooked brown rice and tofu.

SERVES 4

2 teaspoons cornstarch

2 tablespoons toasted sesame oil

3 garlic cloves, peeled and smashed with the flat side of a knife

2 tablespoons (packed) grated fresh ginger

1 medium head cauliflower (about 2 pounds) cut into tiny (1-inch) florets

1 small red bell pepper, veins and seeds removed, diced

3 tablespoons tamari or low-sodium soy sauce

1 cup (about 5 ounces, or 142g) whole roasted and unsalted cashews

$\frac{1}{2}$ cup (150g) diced pineapple

$\frac{1}{3}$ cup (12g) (packed) minced fresh cilantro leaves

In a small bowl, whisk $\frac{1}{4}$ cup (60ml) water with the cornstarch until smooth. Set aside.

Heat a large wok (or large skillet) over medium-high heat. When the pan is hot, add the sesame oil, garlic, and ginger. (Caution: ginger will sputter.) Stir-fry until garlic is fragrant and ginger sizzles, about 1 minute. Add the cauliflower, bell pepper, and tamari or soy sauce, raise heat to high, and stir-fry for 3 minutes. Add the cornstarch slurry (stir with a clean finger to re-dissolve, if necessary) and the cashews and cook until most of the liquid has evaporated and the florets have softened but still retain an al dente bite, about 5 minutes longer, stirring in the pineapple during the last minute of cooking. Sprinkle with the cilantro and serve immediately.

Coconut

If coconuts grew everywhere, the world would be a better place.

Prized for their sweet meat and refreshing liquid (called coconut water), coconuts play a huge role in everything from Thai soups to tanning oils. But when it comes to eating these white-fleshed drupes, many people outside the tropics are more apt to open a can or slit a bag than crack an actual coconut. And while the convenience may be worth it, cracking a coconut isn't tough.

All you need is a hammer, a screwdriver, and a sidewalk. And a coconut.

Tip: To crack and drain a coconut, steady it—eyes up—in a 2-cup glass measuring cup. Hammer a clean Phillips screwdriver through the three eyes. Tip the coconut upside down, draining the water into the cup. Enclose the coconut in a zip-top bag and slam it on the driveway or street. The coconut will crack into several irregular pieces, which you can pry out carefully with a paring knife. Refrigerate the coconut water, covered, and the bag of fresh coconut, separately, until ready to eat.

SIMPLE USES FOR COCONUT:

garnish= grated over frosting, oatmeal, or ice cream
straight up= coconut water after a light workout
piña colada= canned coconut cream + light rum + pineapple juice

Coconut Three Ways

Here's a coconut triple-play: a beverage, *ice cream, and hands-on activity all at once.*

SERVES 6 TO 8

1½ cups (355ml) cold heavy cream

1 cup (240ml) well-shaken coconut milk (do not use "light")

½ cup (120ml) cold whole milk

¾ cup (190g) granulated sugar

½ teaspoon ground cardamom

½ teaspoon almond extract

1 fresh coconut, drained (reserve liquid) and cracked into irregular chunks (see Tip on opposite page)

In a large bowl, whisk the heavy cream, coconut milk, whole milk, sugar, cardamom, and almond extract until the sugar is completely incorporated. (Use the back of a spoon to press out any large cardamom lumps.) Transfer to the frozen base of an ice cream maker and churn according to the manufacturer's instructions. Expect soft-serve consistency only after 30 minutes in the machine. (After 30 minutes, transfer to a freezer-safe container and freeze until ready to serve.)

While the ice cream chills, divide the coconut water among shot glasses. Keep refrigerated.

To serve, scoop the ice cream into bowls. Set a coconut chunk in each bowl, and pass around shot glasses of coconut water. Distribute paring knives so friends can (carefully!) separate the coconut meat from its shell.

Endive

Even if you overlook its fancy French pronunciation (it's ON-deev rather than en-DIVE), this chicory has funny roots, and by roots, I mean roots. Resembling carrots more than lettuces before their tight, leafy heads are snipped off, this bitter winter vegetable makes a sophisticated platform for cold hors d'oeuvre and salads. Or braise or bake it until softened and mellow.

When serving endive leaves at a party, fill their hollows with bits of cheese, creamy dips, or julienned vegetables. You'll get the crunch of a cracker without the fat, salt, or crumbs.

And clean-up's a snap.

Tip: Endive, which comes in deep red and green-tipped white varieties, likes cool, dark environments. Refrigerate in a brown paper bag in your crisper.

SIMPLE USES FOR ENDIVE:

braised endive = endive leaves + butter + water + lemon + stock
salad = endive + pear + goat cheese + candied pistachios + chives + olive oil + sherry vinegar
hors d'oeuvre = endive + diced tangerines + minced olives + crème fraîche

Whipped Gorgonzola Endive with Balsamic Fruits

If chips and salsa bore you, pass around these sophisticated endive spears instead.

When making in advance, sprinkle the apples with lemon juice.

MAKES 16 TO 20 SPEARS

3 ounces (85g) creamy
  (not crumbly) Gorgonzola
  cheese, at room temperature

2 teaspoons milk

1 large head endive, bottom
  trimmed
  and leaves separated

16 to 20 dried cherries

2 to 3 teaspoons aged balsamic
vinegar

$\frac{1}{2}$ small red apple, unpeeled,
cored, and diced

Bring about 1 cup (240ml) water to a boil.

In a stand mixer fitted with the paddle attachment (or with a wooden spoon and some muscle), whip the Gorgonzola until creamy. Scrape down the sides, add the milk, and whip until incorporated. Transfer to a small bowl.

Arrange 16 to 20 endive leaves on a platter.

Place a corresponding number of dried cherries in a small bowl and add boiling water just to cover. Let stand 2 minutes. Drain. Sprinkle the cherries with 2 teaspoons of the vinegar.

Place about 1 teaspoon of the cheese mixture into each endive leaf. Tuck one dried cherry (reserve the vinegar) and 1 cube of apple alongside. Sprinkle the reserved vinegar behind the cheese (so it doesn't brown the apples), adding an additional teaspoon of vinegar, if desired. Serve immediately.

Garlic

Drive through the town of Gilroy, California, on a late July weekend, and your love for garlic will be put to the ultimate test. Unless you suffer from an acute olfactory disorder, you'll immediately know why.

Each summer, this "Garlic Capital of the World" hosts the three-day Gilroy Garlic Festival. With more than 4,000 volunteers, multiple garlic cook-offs, and the annual crowning of Miss Gilroy Garlic, this garlicpalooza has, at times, attracted more than 100,000 attendees.

Garlic undergoes an amazing transformation under heat. Raw, it delivers a bracing, sharp bite, but roast it low and slow in the oven, or sauté it over a barely flickering flame, and it softens and sweetens, turning, with a gentle, heaving sigh, from a tiger to a kitten.

Tip: When chopping garlic, smash it first with the flat side of a heavy knife (stay away from the blade). This forces the garlic to release its pungent oils, adding more flavor to your food.

SIMPLE USES FOR GARLIC:

classic aïoli = garlic + olive oil + salt
soup = a ridiculous amount of roasted garlic + olive oil + butter + stock + cream
pesto = garlic + herbs (basil, or others) + pine nuts + Parmesan + olive oil

Roasted Garlic White Bean Dip with Rosemary Pita

Creamier than hummus, with a mellow sweetness from the roasted garlic, this filling spread can be served warm or cold. You can bake the crisps while the garlic roasts.

·········· **MAKES 1½ CUPS (355ML) DIP AND 48 CRISPS** ··········

1 large head garlic

1 teaspoon plus 1/3 cup (80ml) extra-virgin olive oil, divided

Kosher salt and freshly ground black pepper

1 (6-inch or 15 cm) sprig fresh rosemary, plus 20 plucked rosemary needles

3 (6½-inch or 16.5 cm) rounds whole-wheat pita bread, split in half

¼ teaspoon freshly ground black pepper

1½ cups (420g) cooked white beans, or 1 (15-ounce) can, drained and rinsed

1½ tablespoons fresh lemon juice

Preheat the oven to 350°F (175°C).

Slice off the top fifth of each garlic bulb, discarding the tops. Set the bulbs on a sheet of foil. Drizzle with 1 teaspoon of the olive oil and season with salt. Bring up the sides of the foil and press to close. Roast until very soft, about 1 hour.

Meanwhile, combine the 20 rosemary needles, ½ teaspoon salt, and ⅛ teaspoon pepper in a spice grinder, or use a chef's knife. Grind until powdery.

For the oil, set the rosemary sprig in a small saucepan with the remaining ⅓ cup (80ml) oil. Warm over low heat until the rosemary sizzles and releases its fragrance, about 5 minutes. Let stand off heat for 15 minutes. Discard the rosemary.

Slice the pita halves into eighths, yielding 48 wedges. Divide among two baking sheets. Seasoning one side only, brush first with the rosemary oil, then sprinkle with the rosemary salt. (Reserve the remaining oil.) Bake for 12 to 14 minutes, flipping halfway through and reversing the position of the baking sheets. Remove the pita, and allow the garlic to finish roasting.

When the garlic is ready, remove and carefully open the foil. Cool for 15 minutes, until you can handle it comfortably. Squeeze the roasted garlic from its skin into a food processor. Add the beans, the remaining rosemary oil (reserving 1 teaspoon for garnish), half the lemon juice, ⅛ teaspoon salt, and ⅛ teaspoon pepper and process until smooth. Adjust the seasonings, adding more lemon juice, if desired. Transfer to a small bowl and drizzle with the reserved teaspoon of oil. Serve with the pita crisps.

Jicama

The jicama came out on top. Won the gold. Crushed the competition. A few years ago, a marketing rep from a regional salad bar chain came to my kids' school to lead a fresh vegetable tasting. He piled the students' plates high with vegetables and talked to them about healthful eating.

A quick consensus formed among the under-10 set: out of all the offerings—the carrots and the spinach, the squash and the lettuce, the peppers and the radishes—the students' collective favorite, bar none, was the jicama. The naturally sweet and crunchy sticks seduced nearly all of them, from the burliest fifth graders to the most petite kinderkids. And it's no surprise, really; this juicy tuber is easy to love. It makes an ideal crudité, crunchy slaw, or lunchbox snack. Who needs cheese sticks? Try it with spicy dips. Its cool sweetness offsets heat and acts as a surprisingly effective palate cleanser.

Tip: Removing a jicama's fibrous covering can be a challenge. Your best bet is to use a vegetable peeler, paring knife, or combination of the two to remove the skin.

SIMPLE USES FOR JICAMA:

salsa = diced jicama + red bell pepper + pineapple + black beans + lime + cilantro

dipper = jicama sticks + guacamole

summer roll = shredded jicama + tofu + mango + lettuce + mint + basil + peanuts + rice paper wrappers

Jicama with Peanut Sriracha Dip

With a natural sweetness and decisive crunch, jicama makes an ideal vehicle for scooping up this thick and creamy peanut dip. Add as much Sriracha (a bottled red chili sauce) as you can stand. (Keep in mind that the heat becomes more prominent as the dip chills.)

······················· **MAKES 1 CUP (240ML) DIP AND 30 TO 40 JICAMA SPEARS** ·······················

⅔ cup (160ml) light coconut milk

⅓ cup (80ml) natural peanut butter (crunchy or smooth)

1 tablespoon light brown sugar

1½ teaspoons low-sodium soy sauce

1 teaspoon seasoned rice vinegar

¾ teaspoon fresh lime juice

1 tablespoon grated fresh ginger

1 teaspoon Sriracha sauce, or more, to taste

2 tablespoons finely chopped fresh cilantro

¼ cup (40g) finely chopped unsalted, roasted peanuts, optional

2 medium jicama

Combine the coconut milk, peanut butter, brown sugar, soy sauce, vinegar, lime juice, ginger, and 1 teaspoon of Sriracha in a medium saucepan. Set over low heat and whisk gently until smooth and warm, about 5 minutes. Stir in the cilantro. Cool to room temperature. Transfer to a small bowl and refrigerate, covered, for several hours (or overnight) to allow the flavors to blend.

Meanwhile, peel the jicama with a vegetable peeler, sharp paring knife, or both. (Once you begin peeling, you'll find that you can pull off some of the reedy, fibrous strips of peel with your fingers.) Square off each jicama with a large knife, then cut into sticks roughly ½ inch (1.25cm) wide. Eat any scraps as you go. Refrigerate the sticks, covered, so they're nice and cold.

When ready to serve, taste the dip with a jicama spear to check for heat and balance. (Because the jicama is sweet, tasting them together is important.) Add additional Sriracha, one small squeeze at a time, to achieve your desired heat level. Scrape the dip into a small bowl and serve with the jicama spears.

Tip: This dip would also taste great with carrots, celery, and blanched broccoli. Or toss it through soba noodle bowls with cubes of pan-fried tofu.

Mushrooms

It seems, at times, that the world is divided into two camps: mushroom enthusiasts so passionate about fungi that they a) greet the arrival of morel season with apoplectic glee, and b) devote their weekends, wild-eyed, to foraging in the woods with little more than a bucket, a field guide, and a trusty pocketknife. On the other end of the spectrum, of course, are those who would rather eat paste.

Many of us fall somewhere in the middle. We sauté mushrooms with heaps of garlic, coaxing out their earthy essence, inhaling their musty scent. We stir-fry oyster mushrooms with tofu and long beans, and toss fat Portobello caps on the grill.

We're mushroom lovers with a sustained but tempered passion. We are adherents, we are believers.

We just want others to do our dirty work for us.

Tip: Recently, mushroom foraging has exploded in popularity. Because many fungi are poisonous, always forage with an expert who can keep you safe and help you distinguish the delicious from the deadly.

SIMPLE USES FOR MUSHROOMS:

soup = tofu + shiitakes + rich mushroom stock + green onions + cellophane noodles

portobello pizzas = portobello caps + marinara + basil + mozzarella + Parmesan + olive oil

duxelles = mushrooms + shallots + mixed herbs + butter (serve on toast)

Cremini Farro Hash with Poached Eggs

Farro, a chewy Italian grain gaining in popularity, is a perfect match for meaty mushrooms. When your fork breaks the softly poached egg, the yolk creates an instant sauce that ties all the flavors together.

••• **SERVES 4** •••

1½ cups (300g) semi-pearled farro, rinsed

3 tablespoons olive oil

1 small yellow onion, diced

12 ounces (340g) cremini mushrooms, wiped clean, trimmed, and finely chopped

½ teaspoon dried thyme

Kosher salt and freshly ground black pepper

¼ cup (60ml) dry sherry

1 to 2 tablespoons sour cream, to taste

2 to 3 teaspoons fresh lemon juice

1 teaspoon white vinegar

4 large eggs

3 tablespoons minced chives

Cook the farro in a large pot of boiling, salted water according to package directions. Skim off any foam that rises during cooking. Drain, and rinse.

In a large skillet, warm the oil over medium-high heat. Add the onion, creminis, thyme, 1 teaspoon salt, and a generous grinding of pepper. Sauté until the mushrooms release their liquid, the onions turn translucent, and the moisture nearly evaporates, about 10 minutes, stirring frequently. Add the sherry. Allow to bubble steadily until the liquid nearly boils off, about 2 minutes. Remove from the heat and stir in the farro and sour cream. Season with 2 teaspoons of the lemon juice (adding more to taste) and additional salt and pepper. Cover to keep warm while you prepare the eggs.

Fill a medium saucepan halfway with water. Bring to a hard simmer, add the vinegar, and lower the heat to a gentle bubble. Crack 1 egg into a small ramekin. Swirl a wooden spoon in the water to create a whirlpool, then tip the egg into the swirling water. Immediately repeat with the remaining eggs, nudging the eggs to the side so they don't clump together. Poach the eggs for exactly 3 minutes, flipping them over during the last minute of cooking. (If you're a novice, try poaching 1 or 2 at a time.)

To serve, divide the farro mixture among four serving plates. Remove each egg with a slotted spoon, blot gently with paper towels, and lay atop each mound of farro. Sprinkle with the chives, and serve immediately.

Parsnips

Parsnips don't make life worth living. You must be thinking of pie.

But these late-autumn roots do add a fresh dimension and almost piney sweetness to more popular root vegetables. In fact, if you're a member of the toss-it-all-on-a-sheet-pan-and-roast–until-brown side dish club, and you've yet to add parsnips to the mix, you've been missing out.

Their texture is something of a cross between a carrot and a potato. That said, you can use parsnips pretty much anywhere you'd use a carrot, except on the crudité platter. In a carrot emergency, parsnips could also make a snowman-nose substitute, though given their color they'd be quite tough to see.

Tip: Peel parsnips before use. Also, because their bottoms can be quite skinny, keep a close eye on them during cooking. Caramelization is good; burnt is bad.

SIMPLE USES FOR PARSNIPS:

simple mash = parsnips + potatoes + garlic + buttermilk + olive oil
soup = parsnips + cauliflower + onions + stock + cream + lemon + scallions
roasted side = parsnips + turnips + butternut squash + carrots + red onion + olive oil + rosemary

Thyme-Roasted Parsnips and Pears

*Even though this cold-weather side looks
highfalutin, it takes only minutes to prep.
I like to leave the pears au naturel, with the
peel, stems, and seeds still intact.*

SERVES 4

4 large parsnips (1 to 1½ pounds, or 454g to 680g),
   peeled

2 medium Bosc pears (about 1 pound, or 454g)

1 tablespoon extra-virgin olive oil

1 teaspoon fresh thyme leaves or ½ teaspoon dried,
   plus 1 or 2 sprigs, for garnish (optional)

Kosher salt and freshly ground black pepper

Preheat the oven to 425°F (218°C).

Cut the parsnips in half crosswise at the point where the thicker top becomes narrow and skinny. If the tails are especially thin, toss them on the baking sheet as is. Otherwise, halve them lengthwise. Slice the thicker tops in halves, quarters, or eighths, depending on their width. You're aiming for all the pieces to be relatively uniform. Stand the pears up and slice them in half from top to bottom, leaving the stem intact. Now stand each half up and slice vertically again, creating 4 thick, flat slices (not quarters) of pear. Add to the parsnips.

Drizzle with the olive oil and sprinkle with the thyme, ¼ teaspoon salt, and ⅛ teaspoon pepper. Rub the seasonings in with your fingers and spread the pieces out so they do not touch.

Roast for 25 to 30 minutes, until golden brown and caramelized all over, turning once with a spatula. Garnish with whole thyme sprigs, if desired.

Potatoes

It's a wonder that a hefty baked potato topped with butter, sour cream, and cheese has anything at all in common with a slim, curvy fingerling or a long, crispy fry. But potatoes are tuberous chameleons, so effortlessly able to span the spectrum from low-brow to highbrow, from staple to treat. Ask Mr. Potato Head: he'll tell you it's just as much fun to wear the crazy pink ears as it is to sport the bushy mustache.

Starchy russets were made for baking, their abundant flesh substantial and thick. Waxy Yukon golds mash up into silken purées and take to buttermilk like lint to a pocket. Sweet fingerlings are dainty and demure; when roasted, they're happy to show up in little more than a slip of lemon and a tuft of fresh herb.

It would take the better part of a lifetime to get through the thousands of potato varieties out there. Fortunately, life is long, so I suggest you get started.

Tip: If your potato has started to turn green and sprout, it's still usable, but may be bitter. Carve out the green bits before cooking.

SIMPLE USES FOR POTATOES:

French potato salad = baby new potatoes + crispy shallots + Dijon vinaigrette + chives

tortilla española = Yukon gold or red potatoes + eggs + onions + olive oil

latkes = Shredded russet potatoes + onions + matzo meal + egg + vegetable oil + apple sauce

Gremolata Fingerlings

Potatoes are so often mashed and fried that it's easy to forget they can be
quite elegant, as they are here with a simple topping of lemon, garlic, and parsley.
Of course, some will eat these like French fries, but I'm not naming names.

SERVES 4

2 pounds (907g) small fingerling potatoes, scrubbed and halved lengthwise

¼ cup (60ml) extra-virgin olive oil

Kosher salt and freshly ground black pepper

4 garlic cloves, divided

1 lemon, zest finely shredded, juice squeezed into a small bowl

2 tablespoons minced fresh Italian parsley

Preheat the oven to 400°F (200°C).

Lay the potatoes on a rimmed baking sheet and drizzle with the oil. Season with salt and pepper. Mince 3 of the garlic cloves and sprinkle on the potatoes. Use clean hands to rub in all the seasonings. Spread in a single layer.

Roast until the potatoes are browned and crisp, with tender insides, about 30 to 35 minutes total, flipping with a spatula every 10 minutes. (Cook time may vary as fingerling potatoes can diverge in size, so check them frequently.) The potatoes should face cut side down during the final few minutes of roasting.

Mince the remaining clove of garlic. Add it to a small bowl with the lemon zest and parsley. Stir to combine. (This is the gremolata.)

To assemble, drizzle the roasted potatoes with lemon juice to taste, and transfer them to a serving platter. Sprinkle with the gremolata. Serve.

Turnips

According to Harold McGee in his compre-hensive book *On Food and Cooking*, turnips were among the few dietary staples of primitive Europeans, along with onions, radishes, cabbages, wheat, beans, and peas. If you had a time machine, I'm not sure primitive Europe is the first place you'd go.

But why not? Man can't survive on avocados and toma-toes alone. Our species thrives because we've learned to glorify modest foods—caramelizing onions, smearing radishes with butter, turning wheat into crust, pickling cab-bages, baking beans, and playing with peas.

That leaves us with turnips. Roast them in the oven, braise them gently, or pickle them in brine. Turnips also have a marvelous ability to lighten potato-based dishes, as I've done here. For novices, that may be the easiest way to board the turnip train.

Tip: Old turnips can turn bitter, so eat them on the fresher side.

SIMPLE USES FOR TURNIPS:

side = turnips + celery root + onions + green apple + rosemary + olive oil

early spring stew = baby turnips + baby carrots + asparagus tips + fresh peas + barley + stock

basic glazed turnips = very young turnips cut into coins + butter + nutmeg

Turnip and Yukon Gold Purée with Buttermilk and Chives

The best way to eat turnips is to pair them *with creamy potatoes. The potatoes provide heft, the turnips lend delicacy, and the result is a beautifully balanced purée. Buttermilk adds a pleasant tang; use more, or less, to taste.*

SERVES 6

4 to 6 medium turnips (about $1\frac{1}{2}$ pounds, or 680g)

6 to 8 medium Yukon gold potatoes (about 2 pounds, or 907g), peeled, cut in $\frac{3}{4}$ inch dice

Kosher salt and freshly ground black pepper

3 tablespoons butter

$\frac{1}{2}$ to $\frac{3}{4}$ cup (120ml to 180ml) low-fat buttermilk, to taste

Snipped fresh chives, for garnish

Quarter each turnip. You'll see a creamy, pale yellow ring a few millimeters from the peel. Use a paring knife (instead of a vegetable peeler) to peel the turnips, discarding the ring and everything beyond it. Cut the turnips into $\frac{3}{4}$-inch (2cm) dice and add to a large saucepan with the potatoes. Cover with cold water. Add 1 teaspoon salt and bring to a boil.

Boil over medium-high heat until the vegetables are completely soft, 10 to 15 minutes, skimming off any foam that rises to the surface. Drain.

Fit a food mill over your saucepan and "mill" the vegetables back into the pan. (Alternately, use a ricer or a potato masher.) Whisk in the butter and $\frac{1}{2}$ cup (120ml) of the buttermilk over low heat until the butter melts and the purée is very hot. Add more buttermilk to taste. Season with $1\frac{3}{4}$ teaspoons salt and $\frac{3}{4}$ teaspoon pepper, or to taste, and sprinkle with the chives. Serve immediately.

Sources & Resources

Paulette and I are both big proponents of farmers' market shopping and encourage you to support these markets in your local community whenever possible. However, because geography and climate may limit your access to such markets year-round, we encourage you to procure produce however you can. If circumstances allow you to buy organic, consider doing so.

Here are some companies and organizations whose products and work we support as well. We hope you'll check them out.

MELISSA'S PRODUCE
Melissa's is a large distributor of specialty produce. In addition to exotic varieties of fruits and vegetables, the company also sells a huge array of common produce items, along with many organic options. Melissa's fruits and vegetables can also be found in the produce aisles of grocery stores nationwide.
www.melissas.com
toll-free: 1-800-588-0151

BOB'S RED MILL
Fruits and vegetables are good buddies with grains, especially whole grains, and Bob's Red Mill has some of the best whole grains around. You can find their products in grocery stores or via mail-order. Our favorite products include their polenta, steel-cut oats, bulgur, farro, almond meal, and wheat berries, all of which we feature in this book.
www.bobsredmill.com
toll-free: 1-800-553-2258

MEATLESS MONDAY
The nonprofit initiative Meatless Monday is a terrific resource for those looking to reduce their meat consumption. The site is filled with recipes, articles, and nutritional information,

and works closely with the Johns Hopkins Bloomberg School of Public Health's Center for a Livable Future.
www.meatlessmonday.com

FRUITS & VEGGIES, MORE MATTERS
A health initiative of the Produce for Better Health Foundation, More Matters disseminates information on the benefits of fruit and vegetable consumption and includes links to fruit and vegetable nutrition databases.
www.fruitsandveggiesmorematters.org

LOCAL HARVEST
A comprehensive website that helps consumers find farmers' markets, family farms, and Community Supported Agriculture (CSA) programs near them, with a database searchable by zip code.
www.localharvest.org

SLOW FOOD INTERNATIONAL
A global nonprofit dedicated to promoting good, clean, and fair food grounded in regional traditions.
www.slowfood.com

EDIBLE COMMUNITIES PUBLICATIONS
An award-winning network of publications throughout the United States and Canada devoted to food and farming, and to connecting consumers to the growers in their local areas.
www.ediblecommunities.com

Bibliography

Bittman, Mark. *How to Cook Everything Vegetarian*. New York: John Wiley & Sons, Inc., 2007.

Davidson, Alan. *The Oxford Companion to Food*. New York: Oxford University Press, 1999.

Elia, Maria. *The Modern Vegetarian*. New York: Kyle Books, 2009.

Fletcher, Janet. *Eating Local*. Sur La Table. Denver: Andrews McMeel, 2010.

Herbst, Sharon Tyler. *The New Food Lover's Companion*. Barron's Educational Series, Inc., 2001.

———. *The New Food Lover's Tiptionary*. New York: William Morrow, 2002.

Kamman, Madeleine. *The New Making of a Cook*. New York: William Morrow and Company, Inc., 1997.

Keller, Thomas. *Ad Hoc at Home*. New York: Artisan, 2009.

Kunz, Gray and Peter Kaminsky. *The Elements of Taste*. New York: Little, Brown & Co., 2001.

McGee, Harold. *On Food and Cooking*. New York: Simon & Schuster, 1984.

Page, Karen and Andrew Dornenburg. *The Flavor Bible*. New York: Little, Brown and Company, 2008.

Rogers, Ruth and Rose Gray. *The Café Cookbook*. New York: Broadway Books, 1998.

Terry, Bryant. *Vegan Soul Kitchen*. New York: Da Capo Press, 2009.

Thomas, Cathy. *Melissa's Everyday Cooking with Garden Produce*. New York: Wiley, 2010.

———. *Melissa's Great Book of Produce*. New York: Wiley, 2006.

Vassalo, Jody. *My Cooking Class Vegetable Basics*. Ontario, Canada: Firefly Books Ltd., 2010.

Waters, Alice. *The Art of Simple Food*. New York: Clarkson Potter, 2007.

———. *Chez Panisse Fruit*. New York: William Morrow Cookbooks, 2002.

Whole Living Magazine, eds. *Power Foods*. New York: Clarkson Potter, 2010.

Williams-Sonoma. *Cooking from the Farmers' Market*. San Francisco: Weldon Owen, 2010.

Index